Advance Praise for *The Marriage-Friendly Prenup*

I spent over 30 years mediating hundreds and hundreds of divorces before I began helping couples negotiate their prenups, and what immediately struck me was how the lawyer-driven process of creating prenups almost *guaranteed* that the marriage would end in divorce. Laurie Israel has written a brilliant, much-needed book with detailed, practical advice that shows couples how to avoid this result and negotiate in ways that actually strengthen their marriage. It is not only legally, but financially and emotionally sophisticated, and covers all the most important topics — it is a genuine classic and deserves a place of honor on every bookshelf.

> — Kenneth Cloke, Mediator and author of *The Magic in Mediation: A Search for Symmetries, Metaphors, and Scale-Free Practices*, Santa Monica, California

I wish I had this book 25 years ago. Laurie's analysis of the prenuptial process is methodical, thorough, insightful and revolutionary. It adds humanity and generosity of spirit to the inherently emotionally complex and traditionally purely money-focused process. It helps bring collaborative law and mediation squarely into the prenuptial process. Laurie's style is easy to read, rendering an otherwise heady legal topic accessible to lawyer and lay person alike. Any couple considering a prenuptial agreement or lawyer involved in a prenuptial agreement should read this book.

> — Oran Kaufman, Esq., Attorney/Mediator, Amherst, Massachusetts

The Marriage-Friendly Prenup is the essential manual for any couple considering a prenuptial or postnuptial agreement. The conventional wisdom is that prenups and postnups destroy trust, foment conflict, and complicate a loving relationship. In this book, author Laurie Israel turns that conventional wisdom on its head and explains how frank discussions and wise agreements can strengthen a marriage. Laurie is hands-down the most knowledgeable person on the planet regarding prenups and brings to this important work vital experience as a mediator and collaborative law attorney, with expertise in real estate, tax, and estate planning. This is the book I will be recommending to all of my prenup and postnup clients.

— David A. Hoffman, Esq., Founder, Boston Law Collaborative, LLC and Lecturer on Law, Harvard Law School, Boston, Massachusetts

In her brilliant book, *The Marriage-Friendly Prenup*, Laurie Israel provides a guiding light for informed couples who wished to plan their marriage and finances for a stable, happy, and productive marriage together. Viewing premarital agreements as foundations for successful marriages, or at worst, prevention against litigation that could harm each other and their children, Laurie helps spouses to be the best people they can be, even better than before they set out on their paths to learning about and creating prenuptial agreements. Eschewing the lawyer mantra that both parties should be unhappy after a negotiation, the chapter "Is There a Way to Make Both Parties Happy" should be required reading for clergy, family therapists, lawyers, accountants, and of course, people planning their marriages.

As engaged couples are increasingly hiring progressive family professionals who utilize mediation and collaborative teams to create these agreements, this book should be a guidebook to ensure that the feelings and common values that bring couples together are enacted in their preparation for a successful marriage.

— Forrest S. Mosten, Esq., Mediator and Collaborative Family Law Specialist, Co-Founder of Mosten Guthrie Online Training Academy for Mediation, La Jolla, California

If you, or someone you love, hopes to enter into a healthy marriage — gift them this book! Whether or not they plan to have a prenup, the thought-provoking questions and real life stories shared by Laurie Israel about marriage and prenups can only help. Too many people approach prenups, and marriage, without examining what they are willing to give to a marriage, and what they hope to get from a marriage. With a clarity and grace that comes from years of experience helping couples through the pain of divorce, and now, more joyfully, helping couples create healthy prenuptial agreements, Laurie Israel shares her insightful, optimistic, and grounded wisdom on building a strong, healthy marriage, with, or without, a prenup.

— Karen Van Kooy, Collaborative Lawyer, Mediator. Skylark Law & Mediation, P.C., Southborough, Massachusetts

Prenups are inherently complex emotional and legal processes that need to be done with intentional thought. Laurie gives both an enticing and thoughtful approach to these situations with years of expertise. If you are in a position where you are considering a prenup, make sure you don't skip over this resource!

— Nathan Astle, Marriage and Family Therapist and Certified Financial Therapist, Kansas City, Missouri

Laurie Israel has written a wise, compassionate and insightful guidebook for future spouses contemplating their lives together and contemplating a prenuptial agreement. Her approach is based on a simple observation: since dynamics around money are inseparable from other interpersonal dynamics, a poorly negotiated prenup can easily cause such damage it becomes a tearful roadmap for divorce. *The Marriage-Friendly Prenup* explains how — in the right circumstances, negotiated the right way and with the right terms — a well-crafted prenuptial agreement can actually contribute to the glue that holds a marriage together. Anyone with good reason to go down the prenup path can benefit from the decades of experience Laurie has distilled into her new book.

— Jeffrey Fink, Esq. Kerstein, Coren & Lichtenstein, LLP, Wellesley, Massachusetts

If you believe in the beauty, challenges and complexities of family relationships, and want to support couples to thrive, not just survive, this book is a must-read. It's a vital resource for couples at all stages of their relationship — and for the family lawyers, financial advisors and couples' therapists who can support them. Laurie Israel offers narratives, thought-provoking questions and encouraging tips for sustaining and nourishing relationships. As a Canadian divorce lawyer and mediator, I share the author's disdain for boilerplate "risk management" prenups, drafted without any meaningful discussion about the particular couples' needs and hopes. This book will benefit all families. Thank you for writing it, Laurie Israel!

— Jacinta Gallant, Collaborative Lawyer and Mediator. Author of Going Steady Toolkit and creator of Designing Our Future Together, Charlottetown, Prince Edward Island, Canada.

Laurie's understanding of the nuances needed in the prenup to cover complex financial issues in high-net worth divorce, involving a business valuation, is superb. She identifies the significant valuation and emotional issues facing legacy companies. This book guides the couple through how to equitably handle the profit or growth in value over the marriage and reasonably agree to something that benefits the family, even in divorce. Ideal resource for any couple getting married.

— Melissa Gragg, Bridge Valuation Partners, LLC. Divorce
Financial Mediator and Business Valuation Expert Witness.
St. Louis, Missouri

My dear, departed mentor who practiced family law at the highest level in California for 46 years told me the following when we first discussed prenuptial agreements: "A prenup is always the first pleading prepared in a divorce." In other words, a prenuptial agreement foreshadows an almost inevitable marital dissolution. It does not have to be so.

Laurie Israel's *The Marriage-Friendly Prenup* offers a paradigm shift: Prenuptial Agreements that promote thoughtful, collaborative planning of a couple's financial future. I have personally reviewed far too many prenups designed to ensure one spouse gets to protect their (or their family's) assets while paying the other spouse as little alimony for the shortest time possible.

In Chapters such as "Prenups for Children of Wealthy Parents" and "The Importance of Contribution and Generosity in Marriage," Laurie Israel brings common sense compassion to the subject of prenups for both clients and practitioners. I cannot recommend this book highly enough and plan to use it in my practice.

— Leslie A. Ryland, Esq, Schaffer Family Law Group, San Diego,
California

With her wonderful new book, *The Marriage-Friendly Prenup*, Laurie Israel helps all readers, professionals and «ordinary people» alike, to understand that the process and terms of a couple's prenup will reverberate, for good or bad, throughout one›s marriage. Laurie helps us to understand that the more thoughtful and optimizing the prenup, the greater the likelihood of both a marriage working out and of doing so in optimizing ways. Simply put: the prenup sets the tone for a marriage. Laurie helps us to understand how to most capably set that reverberating tone.

> — Jim Melamed, Founder and General Counsel for Mediate.com and ODR.com

Laurie Israel's second book on prenups features more of her innovative mix of wisdom and practical advice that made her original book such a groundbreaking work in the field. In this accessible, succinct, and surprisingly happy book, Laurie asks the reader to respect the existing laws on marriage and divorce by understanding them, and not as "the enemy" but as a guiding template to creating a healthy prenuptial agreement. The many concerns and creative options so perceptively explored in *The Marriage-Friendly Prenup* are increasingly available to same-gender couples contemplating marriage.

> — Charles Spiegel, Esq. Mediator and Collaborative Practitioner, San Francisco, California

Laurie Israel's *The Marriage-Friendly Prenup* challenges the traditional, adversarial approach to prenuptial agreements. Instead, she advocates for a more compassionate and collaborative process that prioritizes open communication and mutual respect. By acknowledging the emotional complexities of prenups and emphasizing the value of both financial and non-financial contributions, Laurie provides couples with a practical framework for creating agreements that strengthen, rather than weaken, their relationships. Whether you're a couple considering a prenup or a professional working with couples, this book offers valuable insights into building a more secure financial future together.

> — Megan McCoy, Ph.D., Assistant Professor Personal Financial Planning, Kansas State University

I was delighted to feature Laurie Israel on my modernhusbands.com podcast as the leading expert on the uses and misuses of prenups. In her new book, *The Marriage-Friendly Prenup*, Laurie writes engagingly about how to take a thoughtful and compassionate route towards constructing an equitable prenuptial agreement. Building on a sweeping overview of the development of laws of marriage and divorce over time, Laurie moves on to the modern innovation of the prenuptial agreement, which can do major harm if done wrong. This book digs us out of the era of marriage-weakening prenup-pushing and spiritedly charts a new way forward. Done right, prenups can be both marriage-friendly and marriage-bolstering. Any couple thinking about whether or not to get a prenup should read this book. This is absolutely essential reading for every modern husband and modern wife.

> — Brian Page, Founder, "Modern Husbands" website

History and tradition suggest marriage is the ultimate romantic expression. Many older couples, however, hesitate to tie the knot because of the legal implications. Laurie Israel's book, especially her chapter on "gray" prenups, offers solid advice for building a happy life with a new spouse while honoring commitments to kids and grandkids from previous relationships.

> — Laura Stassi, host of the podcast "Dating While Gray: The Grown-Up's Guide to Love, Sex, and Relationships," and author of *Romance Redux: Finding Love in Your Later Years*

The Marriage-Friendly Prenup rightly views a prenup as "a financial plan for a marriage." When a couple approaches a prenuptial agreement with this viewpoint, it takes out the stigma typically associated with prenuptial agreements and allows a couple to have a frank, open discussion about money and the kind of economic partnership they are creating with their marriage. Laurie Israel's new book surveys the various issues a couple should consider when discussing terms for a prenuptial agreement, and provides helpful tips to ensuring not only a successful financial plan, but a successful marriage.

> — Elizabeth S. Warner, Esq., Partner, Pryor Cashman, LLP, New York, New York

THE MARRIAGE-FRIENDLY PRENUP

HOW TO CREATE A THOUGHTFUL AND
CARING PRENUPTIAL AGREEMENT

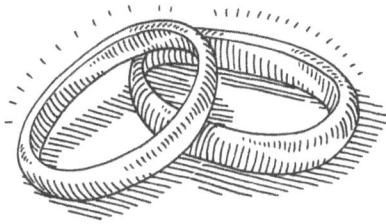

LAURIE ISRAEL

Integrity Registry Press
P.O. Box 73
Plainfield, MA 01070

ISBN 978-0-9998287-2-4
eBook 978-0-9998287-3-1

Cover and book design by Barbara Aronica
Cover illustration by Frank Ramspott
Author photo by Ben Israel and Gabriela Franco Peña

Manufactured in the United States of America

For Elaine and Ben

CONTENTS

INTRODUCTION

This book, *The Marriage-Friendly Prenup: How to Create a Thoughtful and Caring Prenuptial Agreement*, is a concise and updated version of my 2018 book, *The Generous Prenup: How to Support Your Marriage and Avoid the Pitfalls*. This new book offers couples considering prenuptial agreements, as well as their friends and families, guidance on how to handle the pressures and issues caused by prenups, whether one is only being contemplated or is already underway.

The Marriage-Friendly Prenup presents options for the best ways to customize prenups to address many different situations. It explains how important it is to look into the future when formulating one. It also describes dangerous terms in prenups that don't value the contributions of each spouse appropriately. *The Marriage-Friendly Prenup* suggests terms that can make both parties to a prenup feel happy and secure, thereby fostering contentment in the marriage they are about to enter.

I begin this book with descriptions of some of the problems caused by prenups and the primary factual situations leading people to want to have prenups. This is followed by some general information about prenups, marriage, and what happens when you marry without a prenup. *The Marriage-Friendly Prenup* then focuses on several specific prenup issues, such as prenups when a spouse is actively working in their own business, "gray" prenups for second marriages, and prenups for children of wealthy parents.

Prenups, by their very nature, are complex and are affected by various areas of substantive law. To understand prenups and how they can change the way in which or the degree to which certain laws surrounding marriage are applied, one needs to know what those laws are. This book covers much of this material. It also identifies some of the dangers surrounding certain terms that are often heedlessly (and needlessly) included in prenups. This book also includes many possible terms and provisions that can reduce the potential damage of prenups and can help nurture marriages.

Additionally, this book contains ideas and guidance that can mitigate the harm caused by the usual process of *getting* a prenup, which itself tends to be extremely corrosive and sometimes even ends an engagement. It addresses optimal ways to lessen the damage when a prenup is needed and will guide you on finding a suitable prenup attorney, why mediation is often the best first step, and how to find a good prenup mediator.

And finally, *The Marriage-Friendly Prenup* will help you decide whether or not having a prenup is a good idea for you and your marriage.

I hope you enjoy the ride!

–*Laurie Israel, November 2024*

CHAPTER 1:

THE PRENUP MYTH
AND WHY I CHANGED MY
MIND ABOUT PRENUPS

It's March, and it's wedding season for prenuptial agreement attorneys. People are in love and are preparing for their upcoming summertime weddings.

It is five o'clock on a Friday afternoon. I'm in the office wrapping up some work before the weekend when I receive a phone call from a young woman — let's call her Stacey Smith. She says she is supposed to be exchanging vows with her fiancé, John, in three months. John has just told her that he will not get married without a prenup and that his attorney has drawn one up. John says he'll give it to her in a few days, and he wants her to look at it as soon as it arrives.

Although there had been some rumblings about this notion in the past, Stacey thought that John had abandoned the idea of a prenup. After all, John and Stacey became a couple in their junior year of college and have been for the five years since. Meanwhile, the wedding has been planned, and the invitations are stamped and ready to go. The "hold the date" emails have been sent. Stacey and her family are now distraught and angry. In fact, her parents are outraged at John. They have totally lost respect for him for even having considered such a thing.

This scenario is typical of how my first interaction with a prenup client begins. For the clients, it's not a very good way to start a marriage. It sets up a dynamic where the future spouses find themselves in an adversarial situation. And this happens right before the wedding. When attorneys get involved, the situation usually gets worse, and positions become intractable. Often the couple has been in a relationship for several years, so terminating the relationship at this point is generally not an acceptable option for either party. So now what?

People may think it's fair to maintain separate economic assets and income in a marriage. But as most people in long-term marriages will tell you, money and finances are an integral part of a marriage, and they become even more important as time goes on. Providing financial security to a loved one, just as providing comfort and a good meal, is important to the maintenance of a loving bond.

Because of the power of the internet, many people are falling for the hype that prenuptial agreements are necessary for all marriages. But in fact, prenups are overused, are negotiated in a painful way, are often unnecessary, and can be extremely destructive. Many attorneys have bought into the hype as well and relentlessly perpetrate prenups as a necessary premarital step for their clients. They describe the agreement primarily as a vehicle for "risk control." They fail to see how it might negatively affect the health of the marriage.

Marriages with prenups (especially in first marriages) often begin with lingering memories of harsh negotiations by dueling attorneys that may never be forgotten. Many spouses who are a party to prenups feel they've been taken advantage of. They believe that their initial vision of what their marriage would be like when they said "yes" has been damaged. The process can also harm the more-moneyed spouse, making them feel guilty about being a bully, and maybe starting to even feel that they, indeed, are one.

The most common myths about prenups are that they are necessary, that they improve marriages, and that they are a fair way for spouses to deal with each other, especially regarding finances. In my experience, they usually are not. These reasons are myths, not realities. This is what I call the "prenup myth," the hype that prenups are always a good thing and that every marriage should have one.

In fact, they are generally unnecessary (especially in first marriages) and often have the opposite effect than was intended. They detract from marriage because they are often simply unfair and serve to drive spouses apart.

When I was a young attorney, I didn't reflect much on the results of sending a young client (male or female) into a marriage with a typical generic prenup. Only one basic template existed at the time. That template, often still used, specified that any potential financial sharing during the marriage would be at the discretion of the more-moneyed spouse. Also, there would be no guaranteed inheritance rights, even if the marriage remained intact until the death of one spouse many years in the future. These types of provisions persist in many prenups to this day.

In using the off-the-shelf template I found in my forms book, I believed I was following good legal practice. But I didn't comprehend fully at that time what marriage was in its totality, particularly a long-term marriage. I simply did not understand the financial and personal implications of what I had drafted. Simply stated, I didn't understand the harm I was causing.

As I matured and became more experienced in the law and in life, I began to realize more fully the importance of what financial sharing and security assurances meant to the health of a long-term marriage — especially for young people embarking on a first marriage. I started thinking about prenups in a different way, and my drafting and interactions with clients reflected this new approach.

Most prenups are inequitable at the onset of a marriage and become more unfair as time goes on. They can create corrosiveness that will run through all aspects of a marriage. They have the potential to fray the bond that people have developed when entering a marriage at the time when they make a lifelong commitment to each other. But done under the appropriate circumstances (in cases where they truly are warranted), and with fairness and generosity, prenups can also have a positive impact on a married couple. That is the premise of this book and that's why it is titled *The Marriage-Friendly Prenup*.

At its basis, this book is about marriage and money. Despite what newlywed couples might prefer to believe, marriage and money are inextricably intertwined. Money and security (both emotional as well as financial) are crucial to a healthy marriage. Financial issues are known to be the cause of many marital breakups. Prenups at the start of a marriage have the potential and power to distort and weaken the marital relationship.

The flip side of this is that a couple's ability to equitably resolve financially based marital issues during their marriage, or before the marriage if they are negotiating a prenup (if a prenup is necessary), is a key factor in having a successful and loving marriage. Bad prenups can create bad marriages and can lead to divorce. Good prenups (used in the appropriate circumstances) can actually help a marriage.

Unfortunately, many prenups are, in my opinion, insensitively created in their content and process, and are destructive. As this book will reveal, prenups often distort the economics of marriage and can thus have a detrimental effect on a couple.

Of course, marriage is about more than just money. But along with the other things marriage provides, money and financial security are an important part of the bedrock of most marriages, particularly first marriages of relatively young people. I wrote this book because I believe in marriage, and I want to help people beginning their marriages make them as healthy and satisfying as possible.

Although the ongoing media blitz makes it seem that everyone should have a prenup before marrying, it is simply not true.

Prenups are most appropriate for four basic types of couples: the wealthy or people with wealthy parents; older people who are remarrying, especially those with children from a previous marriage; people with significant premarital assets; and people who are engaged actively in a business they own. My view is that people of more modest means, especially younger couples entering a first marriage, do not need a prenup at all. In fact, if asked to prepare one, I decline the assignment, and I may try to talk the person out of the idea altogether.

These days some people may wonder whether they should get a prenup even when there is not a good reason for it. They may become very anxious about the prospect of getting a prenup, especially when those they care about and trust are telling them that they should have one. In some instances, a financial planner or a similar advisor may raise the issue. Nonetheless, on account of the potential downsides of prenups, it is important to determine carefully whether such an agreement might actually be right for you.

The idea that everyone should have a prenup to ward off disaster reminds me of something I read years ago. It was written by Elsie Lincoln Benedict in series of books entitled *How to Get Anything You Want*. The author was a celebrated public lecturer in the early part of the twentieth century. She made her living by giving inspirational talks throughout the country. You might call her an early self-help guru.

After one of her public talks, an elderly man came up to her and said, "I've had lots of troubles in my life, but most of them never happened."

Similarly, a prenup often protects against things that may never happen. It has the downside potential for muddying the waters of a marriage. It ironically often *causes* bad things to happen, such as the breakdown of a marriage. Therefore, if needed, a prenup should be used sparingly, thoughtfully, and creatively. How to think about and create a prenup — when it's needed — is the message of this book.

CHAPTER 2:

DON'T BELIEVE WHAT THE MEDIA OR "SHADOW PARTIES" ARE TELLING YOU

Prenuptial agreements always seem to be in the news these days. More people are considering prenups before marrying. But there are many reasons for people to reject having prenups. However, this latter concept is not strongly reflected in the media.

Recently there has been a special push in the media toward millennials and Gen-Zers to convince them to get prenups, no matter what their actual situation is. Prenups are advocated in the media like candy to a child, touting them as the next best thing for a marriage. Articles such as "Why I Decided to Get a Prenup — and So Should You" and "Here's Why Every Couple Should Get a Prenup Before Marriage" abound in the mainstream media and are read hungrily (and believed) by a vast amount of the public. Such commentaries and reports advise readers that "it is crucial for couples embarking on marriage to have a prenup — or at least consider getting one."

This type of web-based information cultivates an overall interest in prenups, resulting in more people thinking more often about whether they should have one before they marry. One might reasonably call it "fake news." They start to think almost everyone has one, so why not them?

Lately, individual attorneys and law firms have also boarded the prenuptial (and postnuptial) agreement bandwagon. One law firm, for instance, phrases it this way:

"A prenuptial agreement is a smart financial planning tool. A marriage is not just a physical, mental, and emotional union, but a financial one too. Entering into a prenuptial or postnuptial agreement can provide a sense of security couples require."

Another firm states the following:

"Consider us your trusted legal advisor. We'll meet your need to ensure this matter is taken care of — so you can move forward with your wedding day without worry, concern, or regret later. There is no obligation after that first meeting with us. But you deserve to think through your situation before rushing into the next chapter of your life."

This reinforces the idea bouncing around the internet that more people are considering having prenups. Attorneys are now reporting a marked increase in interest. That seems to be a real chicken-and-the-egg situation. The selling of prenups in the media as the be-all and end-all cure for a possible bad marriage, and hence a bad divorce, creates a self-fulfilling prophecy. People are starting to be more interested in considering having one.

But this media frenzy promotes prenups with little thought as to what changing the financial terms of the marriage might do to the physical, mental, and emotional health of a couple. This is what this book is largely about.

Aside from attorneys promoting their services to "protect" marriages, oftentimes a business associate or an estate-planning advisor will strongly suggest a prenup to an engaged person. Or, perhaps, it's a financial planner who took a continuing education course in which an expert told them that prenups are necessary in every marriage. Or it's a family member with a bad divorce experience who might encourage an engaged relative to get one. I've heard of many divorced clients complaining that "she (or he) got half of my assets." That's ironic, as this is the appropriate result in most long-term marriages. We call these third-party advisors "shadow parties."

Sometimes the professionals advising a client to get a prenup are young and have no experience in long-term marriages. In many instances, they themselves have no such agreements in their own marriages. But invariably, they feel compelled to suggest one to their clients because they were taught that prenups provide "risk containment." They believe that they are not serving the client well if they don't recommend one. Or maybe the advisor had been in a marriage that ended in divorce, and they feel burned. They believe things would have been better for them if there had been a prenuptial agreement. So, they feel compelled to encourage their client to have one.

Invariably, these "advisors" are insensitive to the negative dynamics and memories that even negotiating a prenup can generate. In almost every prenup I see with young people marrying, tears are shed during the process. One person feels unloved and starts to question the commitment of their future spouse. They wonder if they should have ever agreed to marry that person, or even to have been in a relationship with them. The other person feels insecure and fearful of going into a marriage without financial protections. Actually, signing a prenup can be worse, because the economic terms imbedded in them often have a strong potential to upset the balance of fairness and mutual support in the upcoming marriage.

"Risk containment," "risk management," and "asset protection" are interesting terms as they relate to prenups and ultimately marriages. Many advisors are touting these as reasons to have a prenup. The meaning and goal of risk management is to prevent loss of financial assets for the benefitted future spouse.

However, there is another way to articulate the significance of these terms. An unbalanced and unfair prenup can jeopardize the marriage itself. Financial risk containment for one spouse in a prenup might unfairly affect the security of the other spouse. Ironically, this might pose great risk to the ultimate success of the marriage. It comes down to the all-important question in every case: What's more important, the money or the marriage? A good prenup generally encompasses a delicate balancing act between the two.

CHAPTER 3:

THE PROBLEM WITH PRENUPS

Prenups can be helpful to marriages and may be needed to create fairness and peace within the upcoming marriage. But they may also cause unintended harm. There are many reasons for this. Negative dynamics can intensify during the process and negotiations, as well as by the terms that often end up in the prenups themselves.

One problem is that prenups are generally not designed to protect *both* parties entering a marriage. They have historically almost always been one-sided, typically designed to protect the person with greater wealth or income — the "more-moneyed" spouse. These prenups operate almost invariably to diminish the rights that accrue upon marriage of the other spouse. It doesn't sound like a very good deal for the less-moneyed spouse, whose rights are diminished, does it? That's because it isn't. Worsening this is that the prenup process is done at what is usually the most idyllic time in a couple's relationship — right before the marriage.

Usually, there is an element of control involved. A couple gets engaged. They've been with each other a fairly long time. Then one of them suggests (it's really a demand because it's non-negotiable) that they have a prenup. It is difficult for the other to walk away from the relationship that has grown into what they both see as a lifelong marriage. But the law sees it differently — that the person who doesn't want the prenup can just "walk away." Not very realistic, right?

People entering into premarital agreements, unbeknownst to them, are seeking to change the basic rules of money and marriage that have been developed over generations. These rules reflect cultural values and economic morality. They are imbedded in the state laws affecting marriage, divorce, and inheritance. That's what the law is at its core.

People use that as a justification for *having* a prenup. They say, when you marry you have a prenup, anyway, because of the laws that apply to marriage. So why not actually create one for ourselves? Yes, the "law" does in fact, imply a prenup when you marry. But that is not actually a bad thing.

This book is partly about how tampering with the laws of marriage by means of a prenup can often disrupt a couple's values and ideals involving money and marriage. When you sign a prenuptial agreement, you may be altering and destabilizing your marriage. It's not that every prenup is unreasonable, or that they should never be used. There are some good reasons to have one. This book also discusses in what circumstances signing a prenup is a reasonable and rational thing to do. I'll also discuss what can be done to mitigate the damage often caused by prenups, and how to create value for both parties when creating one.

When a loving couple starts to create a prenup, it's usually initiated by one side, the more-moneyed future spouse. The interchange and resulting legal process in getting a prenup negotiated, written, and signed is generally brutal and harsh. You might even call it cruel.

But once this scenario begins, usually in an adversarial atmosphere, the implication is often "marry me with a prenup or not at all." This is a conflict and dilemma going to the very heart of the upcoming marriage. If the future spouse, who doesn't want a prenup, also doesn't wish to face starting all over in another relationship, he or she must now deal with this implied "take it or leave it" ultimatum.

This is not a very loving way to begin a marriage. The parties are now thrust into a tense situation, with emotional and financial ramifications involving their future union that they cannot even imagine or understand, especially if they are relatively young and embarking on a first marriage. They are now dealing with opposing lawyers in a negotiation. (Spoiler alert: young people in love and getting married don't usually want to get enmeshed in contract negotiations with opposing lawyers engaged in and controlling the process.)

Sometimes there are "pro-prenup" attorneys representing the more-moneyed spouse who are very harsh and will brook little or no compromise. They most likely view a prenup as a "business deal." They'll tell the other side that "the prenup can just be tucked away in a drawer" and "hopefully it will be never used."

But marriage is not just a business deal. The future spouse who doesn't want the prenup, or who wants a less extreme one and can't get the other side to budge, is now facing a difficult and blunt choice: Marry me with *this* prenup or do not marry at all. If it's signed, it is likely that it *will* be taken out of the drawer someday.

I have met and heard of very few people who have reached the stage of engagement when a marriage is planned who are willing to abandon the marriage when given this choice. Most engaged couples have made a significant personal investment in their relationship by that time. Often there is a long history of dating; many have cohabited for significant periods of time. They may already be considered members of each other's families of origin. So, if one side caves in and the prenup is signed, its terms will then start to reverberate throughout the marriage itself.

The results can be profound, and the aftereffects of prenups linger in the background of a marriage. Memories of a partner's lack of empathy and generosity can remain embedded in both sides' memories for the entirety of their marriage. Often, I am called to work with couples who signed a prenup that they now want to change because it has caused a corrosive element in their marriage ever since the signing.

A prenup is not a trivial thing. It is of crucial importance. When people are entering into prenups, they are almost always taking away marital rights that a spouse would have under the laws of their state. Otherwise, why enter into one? The rights taken away are often significant property rights. That's why having one needs to be considered very carefully, and if you have one, the terms that are in it — every one of them — are of crucial importance.

Let's say that one future spouse (as is often the case) doesn't want to sign a prenup. That person might believe in a concept of marriage as sharing everything and might perceive the separation of assets and other limitations to sharing as antithetical to this concept. How can that person's values be accommodated when a prenup is presented to him or her? Generally, it cannot.

Can a prenup protect both spouses? Yes, if it's a good prenup. Can a prenup in some ways provide a less financially secure future spouse more (rather than less) than would be provided under applicable state laws? Yes, it can, and a balanced prenup can and should. Are some prenups useful to have in place, and some not? Yes, so consider carefully whether or not you're going to have one.

The drawbacks I discuss here don't apply as strongly to second marriages or for older couples. But there are still drawbacks to prenups in these situations. People need to be aware of the implications involved in structuring the financial affairs of a marriage, even if they are middle-aged or older and are embarking on a second (or third) marriage and especially if they have children from previous marriages. Some of these future spouses need to consider protecting each other financially in their middle-aged or gray marriage as well.

It is reasonable to want to avoid a court battle at the time of divorce. However, I have never seen a prenup that only defines an out-of-court resolution process in case of divorce and does nothing else. This would be the most efficient way to achieve this goal of avoiding litigation. A "legal process prenup" might require the couple to enter negotiations, then mediation, perhaps followed by using a collaborative divorce process, with a final resolution by means of binding arbitration and applying the state's divorce laws within that process. Bingo, you've avoided a long, protracted, expensive (and painful) court divorce process.

When you write a prenup, you are constructing a "private" law to apply to your marriage. This leaves out flexibility for the future, and it also changes the marital relationship. It might change the nature of the marriage itself in ways that were not intended. Uncoupling state law from a marriage by means of a prenup can restrict some possibly better resolutions if the marriage ends in divorce.

Divorce law is reflective of the future. It is flexible. It can determine how to solve the puzzle of a divorce based on facts as they exist at the time of divorce. What if a divorce occurs 25 years after a marriage? What if one of the spouses became a stay-at-home spouse with a part-time career? Should that spouse really have no spousal support, even if the other party can afford it? Should that spouse have no interest afforded in a business that was built up during the marriage? And yet prenups often contain these types of terms.

Divorce laws are (or seek to be) fair and flexible. Yet courts routinely enforce prenups that give a spouse a tiny fraction of what the spouse would be entitled to under state law. Isn't this proof that the deal made in the prenuptial agreement years earlier was unfair to that spouse who is contesting it (or would want to contest it)? Wouldn't you be suspicious that the growing inequality may have caused the marital breakdown?

Many things unforeseeable at the time the prenup is signed will likely happen during the course of a marriage. Applying these state laws at the time of divorce can be more sensible than "making up" the laws at the time of a marriage. If a spouse gets a "better" result than he or she would obtain under state divorce laws, isn't that better result, by definition, unfair and the result of overreaching?

There can be a severe imbalance present and a lack of *quid pro quo* in most of these prenuptial agreements. These imbalances are bound to affect the marriage. After all, why should the spouse who has been cut out of their rightful benefits feel good about it?

Typical prenups drafted by many attorneys are often extreme, especially when they apply to young people embarking on a first marriage. They go far beyond what might be needed to be helpful in certain situations. They become monolithic, passed around in Word documents from law firm to law firm, from lawyer to lawyer. The templates tend to be used repeatedly for all marriages, without much thought. This is the legal equivalent of applying an ax to cut a piece of fish on your plate. Because they are not customized to a particular situation, they often are not reflective of the intent of the future spouses, their particular situations, or their histories.

Often a future spouse may *think* he or she wants a prenup but doesn't understand its effects or implications. That person's attorney may support the client's request without any reflection or discussion. There may be no counseling on the downsides of having a prenup.

There are other obvious drawbacks when couples have signed a prenup.

Prenups can offer a party an easy way out. This means an advantaged spouse may have no "skin in the game." If a spouse gets to keep all their money to themselves, why stay in the marriage when it is experiencing one of a long-term marriage's predictable low spots? Financial interdependency is part of the glue that holds most marriages together. Case in point: the multiple divorces and remarriages of celebrities and rich people.

For most marriages, there is much satisfaction in building up a "financial joint venture," creating comfort and security as the marriage progresses over time and as the couple ages. Prenups can take away the act of collaboration in achieving this goal. Separate property and separate income have a way of pulling people apart — they no longer function as a team.

A related issue affecting marriage when there is a prenup is a lack of excitement that building a financial life together entails. When the results are known and preplanned, and when there is no sense of risk of loss or gain, there is the absence of a certain pleasure of anticipation and achievement. Along with this is a diminishment in the delight in finding a path that has not been preset for you.

As pointed out earlier in this chapter, many people don't really want to sign a prenup if that's the only way they can marry the person they love. On many levels, that's the result of a process that is coercive. However, this sort of coercion does not rise to the legal level of invalidating a prenup. If you sign it, even if you feel coerced and even if it has very adverse provisions to you, you should assume that it will not be invalidated in court.

Here's something I find very irritating. Lots of young internet influencers are telling millennials and Gen-Zers that they must have a prenuptial agreement when they marry. These advisors are usually people who have not been in a long-term marriage — they're too young to have been in one! They have no idea what being in a long-term marriage entails and how a prenup can destabilize one. Yet they are advising others that they should have a prenup!

Another irritant to me is when people are convinced that they need to have a prenup because of the influence of a third party. We call these people "shadow parties." Often, they are people who believed they were "burned" by their divorce or know other people who were "burned" by divorce. When you probe into the divorce terms of those "burned" people, you will almost always find that property accumulated during the marriage was divided equally, which is usually how divorces work all over the country.

Some of these shadow parties are well-off parents who want their children to have prenups to keep their inheritances within the bloodlines. There are other ways that these parents can achieve these goals, and they have no idea how this request can throw a wrench into their child's marriage and both future spouses' relationships with their in-laws. I've seen it happen numerous times.

It's important for attorneys to take a step back and help clients contemplate and keep an open mind as to whether or not a prenup is really necessary. And if it's advisable to have one, it's important to consider with a fresh perspective what kind of prenup it will be and what provisions it will contain.

Unlike what typically comes out of many attorneys' offices, many diverse types of prenups are possible, with multiple options as to their terms. The variations are virtually endless. The more thoughtful and customized a prenup is, the more it will be fair to both parties, and the more likely it will actually be helpful to the upcoming marriage.

This book will describe the various prenup terms that are possible, terms that end up being negative for the marriage, and the optimum process for getting a prenup done.

CHAPTER 4:

PEOPLE WHO MIGHT BENEFIT FROM A PRENUPTIAL AGREEMENT

When a new client comes to me for prenup representation (or an engaged couple, for prenup mediation), it quickly becomes apparent why they might want a prenup. I encounter the same scenarios repeatedly. As attorneys, we call these situations "fact patterns."

For attorneys, a fact pattern is a very important concept. In law school, we are given complex factual situations and are asked to describe how we would address the fictional client's problems by applying the law to those specific facts. This turns out to be good preparation for a career in law, sleuthing through many facts to get to the heart of the matter and find a solution.

About fifteen years ago, aghast at several nasty prenup agreement negotiations in which I had represented clients, I started writing about prenuptial agreements for the general public. One of my earliest articles was entitled "Ten Things I Hate about Prenuptial Agreements." I think people were really impressed because an attorney had written it, and yet it criticized the brutal and insensitive way attorneys often handled prenups. The article went viral. People all over the country are still reading it to this day.

People share with me their experiences (mostly negative, in fact some *very* negative) in going through the prenup process. This process includes negotiation of terms, often causing damage to their once loving relationship — and at a very tender time, right before the wedding. I have been contacted by people who decided to marry with a prenup they thought was very unfair. I also have been contacted by people who decided *not* to marry their fiancé after the other person demanded that they sign what they felt was a very unfair prenup. You might call such a person "prenup jilted."

There are a limited number of types of fact patterns among the clients I meet with. Within each set of fact patterns there are numerous variations. And each couple has their own preferences as to what is fair and workable in their financial plan for their marriage. These make the handling of each case individual. Every prenup should be different. A customized and thoughtful prenup has the potential for doing good for the clients. An off-the-shelf prenup can cause ongoing harm. There is no one-size-fits-all prenup that is beneficial.

Here are some examples of fact patterns that I often see:

1. Marriage occurring in their mid-30s. One party has accumulated substantial assets.

People are getting married later in life than they used to. When they marry, they are often substantially older than their parents' ages when their parents got married. "Delayed" marriage is especially prevalent for professionals, the college educated, and people successful in business. These are the types of people I often work with on prenups. Because of the later marriages, many people already have established careers and have accumulated substantial assets.

This often results in a disparity in the accumulation of assets between the future spouses and differences in earning power and earning potential. It may cause some concern on the part of both spouses. Sometimes the spouse who accumulated the assets did so at great personal cost, by denying themselves disposable income in order to save part of their earnings. I have seen people in their late 30s who have accumulated over a million dollars in assets by the time they marry, without the help of family money, and working in not particularly lucrative careers.

Although this is unusual, it can lead the person who has accumulated the assets to wonder about having a prenup. The other party may wish to be "fair" and not claim rights to that nest egg if the marriage ends in divorce, especially if it turns out to be a short-term marriage. But what happens in a medium-length or a long-term marriage? Should this separation of premarital assets be a rule that affects things 30 years from now? These are reasonable concerns that can be addressed in a prenup that can put each party's mind at ease.

2. One party built up an ongoing business before the marriage.

When someone is engaged in a business that they created, one through which the person derives earnings, it's often a good reason for a prenup. Legitimate concerns about preserving the business can trigger the desire to have the security of a prenup. It's different than being an employee and receiving salary or wages that are reportable on a Form W-2 for tax purposes.

A business (or a portion of it) that a spouse created is often considered a marital asset to be divided in a divorce, if the spouse is actively engaged in that business during the marriage. That includes the value of the business at the time of divorce including any increases in value since the time of the marriage, if the business was started before the marriage.

Another issue to be addressed is what happens to the profits of the business during the marriage. In many closely held businesses, a person's income is simply the taxable profit that the business generates each year. Sometimes, the earnings are characterized partly as the salary of the owner and partly as business profits.

What happens if the salary is set at an artificially low level? Does the net profit in addition to the salary get shared in the marriage? What if the business owner needs (or wants) to reinvest profits back into the business to grow it or to address financial problems that the business is experiencing? What happens to the business at the business-owner's death? What happens to a spouse's interest if the business-owner spouse has other business partners? What happens at divorce? Does the business-owner spouse get to keep control of the business?

These are all important questions that arise and can be addressed in the business-owner prenup situation. Solutions need to be carefully considered and evaluated after open discussion and analysis. (See Chapter 14 for more information.)

3. One party works in their parents' business.

This is a variation of the scenario we just looked at that comes up frequently in my practice.

One party works in their parents' business. That's both the good news and the bad news. The good news is that they make a very good living in a stable family business and (hopefully) enjoy their work. They have very good job security. If everything works out, the parents will gradually let go of control of the business and give (or sell) the business to them, perhaps retaining a passive income interest. After the parents die, presumably their son or daughter would inherit the business. Sometimes the future spouse may be working with their siblings or other family members in the business. The parents, even when active in the business, may be gifting partial business interests to their child/children (or are thinking of doing so soon) as an estate-tax saving strategy.

The parents are self-made people. They started the business right after their marriage. They are concerned that the business stays within the bloodlines. Even though they didn't have a prenup, they started to be concerned when their child told them about their engagement. They are very afraid that if this marriage ends in divorce, the ex-spouse could have a claim on the business assets or income — or worse, a claim for an *ownership* interest in the business. The parents do not want this scenario to play out and want to keep any claims of ex-spouses impossible. The parents are now requesting (really mandating) that there be a prenup before their child marries. Learning this, of course, has had a profound negative impact on their child and their child's future spouse.

There is a legitimate interest in not having an ex-spouse have control in a family business after a divorce. I've seen that nightmare situation happen in marriages that had no prenup when I represented people in divorces. On the other hand, formulating a fair result in a prenup where each party's contribution will be fairly valued, whether in the workplace or in other aspects of life, is important to the health of a marriage.

In these cases, finding an equitable solution is important, because the nonbusiness spouse (especially in a first marriage) is certainly worthy of accumulating financial security as much as the other spouse as time goes on. There are ways to think out of the box, to meet both the family's goals and the new couple's goals and to create fairness within the marital unit and peace within the families of origin.

4. One party's parents are wealthy and want them to have a prenup to protect their inheritance and lifetime family gifts.

This is a frequent fact pattern I see in my practice. It's often referred to as the "shadow party" prenup. A shadow party in legal lingo is someone, not your client, who is influencing, or perhaps directing, the terms of the prenup. Generally, it's the parents of one of the future spouses, or a family advisor or family attorney. If their child doesn't comply with their wishes, the parents can threaten to disinherit them.

Compounding this problem is when the attorney representing the child of the wealthy parents is the parents' business or estate-planning attorney, because the parents directed the child to use that attorney to represent him or her. Who is that person really representing? Or maybe one of the client's siblings has already married and agreed to a very restrictive prenup. In that case, there might be more pressure for the child of wealth to capitulate to the parents' (and their advisors') restrictive terms. On the other hand, if the child of the wealthy parents is the first sibling to marry, that person can set a tradition of generosity.

The less-moneyed future spouse has told their parents about the prenup, because they couldn't keep something so important from them. Their parents are livid. They believe a prenup ruins the trust that a good marriage needs to thrive, and that it also detracts from marriage as a joint venture. The parents of the less-wealthy spouse don't know how they will look the other future spouse's parents in the eyes at the wedding.

Often in these cases, the first draft of the prenup written by the wealthy family's business lawyer or their estate-planning attorney is overly restrictive. It may entail no sharing of assets or of income derived from the family assets whatsoever (even with respect to the child's own separate assets), except to the extent the future spouse wishes to share it. Sometimes it even says that the earned income of the child will be separate property. Sharing would be in the complete control of the moneyed party *forever*, even after death.

This causes an unbalanced situation between the spouses. They need to talk about how they would handle the infusion of wealth from the parents of one of them. It's not something that will go away. It needs to be addressed because it exists. Working this out in the prenup context will be a healthy exercise for the new couple. (For more information on this scenario, see Chapter 13.)

5. "Gray" prenups for later-in-life marriages.

This is one of the best (and most common) reasons to have a prenup, especially if there are children from their previous marriages. People getting remarried later in life have a great sense of loyalty both to their children and to their new spouse, whom they love.

Having a prenup in this situation can be a very good thing. It tends to create peace within the newly extended blended family. Inheritance and money can be addressed in a way that encourages trust and respect, and that reflects the thoughtful wishes of the new couple.

A balanced plan can be made to provide for a new spouse. Also, after the death of a more-moneyed spouse, there can be provisions both for the new spouse to have security (if needed) and the children of the deceased spouse to receive a legacy. Having such a plan in a prenup often eases the acceptance of the new stepparent. It balances the financial loyalty a person has to their children and the concern and love for the new spouse in a reasonable and rational way. (For more on this, see Chapter 15.)

6. People who want to fix a bad prenup.

I work with a number of clients who come to me after their marriage has taken place, perhaps several years afterward. They had a very corrosive prenuptial agreement. Their negotiation process ran very close to the wedding, leaving a huge wound in their relationship. They each had a lawyer, and with the back-and-forths, they just didn't have time to get the terms of the prenup to where they wanted it, but they signed it anyway because the wedding date was approaching.

They were both very angry and sad about the resulting document. They both felt the results didn't reflect their wishes and values. It's caused them problems and has been eating away at them ever since the marriage.

Fixing bad prenups and helping overcome corrosive experiences can be a very important job for a prenuptial agreement attorney or prenuptial agreement mediator. Bad prenups can be fixed and good prenups created. They may have the changes put into effect by creating an amendment to the prenup, or they may opt for a postnuptial agreement (depending on the particularities of state laws to address this situation).

People *can* revise their prenup after their marriage to reflect their current wishes and situations. Sometimes after living together for a while, it becomes quite clear as to what should have been written in the prenup in the first place.

People with prenups also have the power to terminate their prenup completely. This should be done with much thought, and with a formal written agreement signed by both spouses and acknowledged by a notary public. It's best to consult counsel before embarking on this. There are important rights that might be in the existing prenup (including ones that benefit the less-moneyed spouse) that would be lost when a prenup is terminated.

7. People who didn't have time to do a prenup: the "prenup-postnup."

Here's another frequent fact pattern. The wedding date is looming. The prenup is complex or the couple just can't decide on certain issues. They have been working on it (plus doing their wedding planning) for two months. The wedding is two weeks away, and the prenup is still not done. They want to focus on the wedding now and on their joy to be marrying each other, and not think about the prenup. So far, the prenup process has been a horrific experience, which keeps taking them into a bad mental state. They do not want to ruin their wedding over this.

They both agree to put the prenup off until after the marriage. They want to give it a rest. Even though the prenup was initiated by the more-moneyed spouse, each trusts their future spouse to continue the process after the marriage. They rely on the cooperation and good faith of their promise to finish the prenup after their marriage. Now the prenuptial agreement will be called a "postnuptial" agreement. (See Chapter 18 to find out more about postnuptial agreements.)

8. One party got "burned" by a bad divorce.

Their prior marriage of 25 years ended in a protracted, litigated divorce. The legal costs ran into the hundreds of thousands of dollars, and they had to fight to get joint custody of their kids. They are afraid to marry again because of this terrible experience. This is actually a very good reason to have a prenup.

Many prenups (and all the ones I draft) have a robust Alternative Dispute Resolution (ADR) clause in them. It provides that in case of divorce, the couple must avail themselves of various out-of-court

methods of coming to an agreement instead of going to court and lit-
igating. These methods include plain vanilla negotiation, mediation,
case evaluation, collaborative law, and, finally, binding arbitration.

Although courts always have final jurisdiction over the rights of
children, this type of clause goes a long way in preventing the nightmare situation that this potential client faced. A prenup could be written as a "bare bones" one that addresses only this ADR clause.

• • •

These are the major reasons (and good ones) that people come to me to
help them formulate or mediate prenups. There are many variations of
these. You'll find more information on each of them, and how to solve
the puzzle they present, in an effective, humane, and marriage-friendly
manner in the subsequent chapters of this book.

CHAPTER 5:

THE IMPORTANCE OF CONTRIBUTION AND GENEROSITY IN MARRIAGE

One of the major problems with prenups is that they often don't reflect and value the full range of spouses' contributions to a marriage. Many of these contributions are nonmonetary. How can you value parenting, companionship, the creation of a peaceful and beautiful home, or someone who always has your back? Prenups tend to value the financial contributions of the more-moneyed or "earner" spouse more than the nonfinancial contributions of the other spouse.

In virtually all 50 states, the efforts of two spouses in a marriage are deemed of equal value, whether or not these contributions are monetary. The idea is that if both spouses devote their efforts fully in support of the marriage — whether at home or in the workplace — it is considered an equal exchange. When each spouse's efforts are valued by the other, it is an important factor in sustaining a successful, long-term marriage. When one person is contributing 100 percent to the marriage and the other person less than 100 percent (perhaps because their business was designated in a prenup as "separate property"), the marriage may fail due to the imbalance of contributions.

The law reflects this reality. In divorce law in all states, the value of a stay-at-home spouse is considered equal to that of a spouse working outside the home. No one can set a price on the value of a spouse who works in the home, raises children, and often puts a career on hold (with a lifetime effect of negative earnings capacity) to support the earner spouse's career and the family as a whole. No law devalues the work of a spouse who is a schoolteacher with that of the other spouse who is a well-paid investment fund manager. Courts will assume (generally correctly) that the decision to engage in these two disparate careers, offering different public contributions to society, reflected a mutual decision.

And yet, prenups often *devalue* the efforts of the nonearner (or lower-earning) spouse. They often provide mega-protections for the more-moneyed spouse by taking away some important rights of the other spouse. They put the nonearner spouse in a financially precarious position, because the prenup contract takes away the usual financial protections of the law. These protections no longer apply to this spouse. The sting of this devaluation and the negative practical result is felt by **both** parties and typically influences the marriage over time. It creates a wound that may never heal.

That's why you should be careful and thoughtful when you are structuring the financial framework that will govern your marriage in a prenup.

"Contribution to marriage" is a legal term. You see it written in most states' divorce laws. It is a factor when determining property division and spousal support in divorces. The "contribution" concept is further developed in case law. "Case law" is a term that refers to law established through judicial decisions in individual cases, rather than through legislative statutes. The concept of "contribution to marriage" clearly encompasses economic as well as noneconomic contributions.

Let's say that one of the spouses in a marriage leaves the full-time job market to focus on having a family. When they return to the job market a number of years later, it is often part time at first. Even when they return to full-time work, their lifetime earning potential may be compromised. That spouse has relegated their career to second place so they can concentrate on their family, home, and marriage. The splitting of the functions is the way the couple has decided that the marriage and family can benefit as a whole. It is a joint decision.

This situation can work out just fine if the marriage lasts, but what if there is a divorce? State laws assign a value to that change in a spouse's financial prospects. But how can that spouse's contribution be fairly valued if a prenup signed years before the breakup says that it won't be? Prenups that reward financial contributions over family and home-making contributions do just that. If a prenup maintains the value of a spouse's business as separate property and the other spouse is sharing all their efforts as marital property, it is a problem.

In most states, lost economic opportunity is embedded into the law as a factor considered in divorces. A typical state statute provides that the economic *and* noneconomic contributions of both parties to the marriage are to be considered when determining both alimony and property division. Typically, a court will consider occupation, amount and sources of income, vocational skills, employability, length of marriage, and opportunity of each for future acquisition of assets or income as well as other factors when determining property division.

In addition, for purposes of calculating spousal support, courts will typically consider the contribution of a party as homemaker to the family, economic and noneconomic contributions of both parties to the marriage, marital lifestyle, ability of each party to maintain the marital lifestyle, and lost economic opportunity as a result of choices made during the marriage.

Measure this against the provisions contained in many prenups — that the less-moneyed spouse waives spousal support. How does that reflect that spouse's contribution to a marriage? How does that demonstrate love to a spouse at the time of a marriage?

In the law, marriage is viewed as a shared enterprise akin to a financial partnership, in which the parties are equal partners and should share equally in all the results of the marriage, including the financial results.

Here's how one court put it:

> Like a commercial partnership, the parties in a marriage function by sharing duties and by dividing their labor, without which the relationship could not succeed. It is conceded that the relationship cannot successfully operate without the acquisition of some capital. The accumulation of that capital, however, will not occur, especially if children are present, unless the homemaker-spouse contributes a significant part of her energies to the marriage. The services of both are necessary for the continuance of the relationship.

Sometimes litigants in divorce cases try to value the homemaker's efforts by ascribing hourly wage rates to their efforts. A nanny might earn $20 per hour, a cook perhaps $15, and so on. They add these up to quantify the "wages" of a homemaker-spouse.

This method of calculating "wages" is usually not successful in court actions, and for good reason. You cannot place a monetary value on making a home for the family and caring for a spouse. There is a meaningful and profound contribution made by a homemaker and at-home parent to "hearth and home" that is not present when the duties are done by hired help. (This is not meant to disparage dual-party working spouses. That is simply another valid choice spouses can make as a couple.)

One could say that by giving a married couple the ability to have children and raise them is a form of "capital" that our society assigns a value to. This value is equal to the monetary capital that can be earned by the spouse who is now freed up to earn income outside the home and amass property during the marriage. The courts merely reflect and affirm these cultural values. What happens to the marriage with a pre-nup that does not affirm these cultural values? It can cause harm to the marriage. What happens when these values are not put into effect in divorce terms if the couple ends their marriage by divorce? It can cause harm to the disadvantaged spouse.

There are couples who do not have children, either by choice, by circumstance, or because it is a "gray" marriage of middle-aged or older spouses. For these couples also, courts and the laws value a stay-at-home spouse as equal to the earner spouse. The spouse who manages the home life provides an equally important ballast to the activities of the other spouse. The fact that one spouse is not in the workplace (or is working less) is deemed to be a mutually conceived marital decision.

You might characterize contribution as what spouses offer each other in a marriage. Contribution may also be characterized as spouses acting in the spirit of generosity. That makes *generosity* a close cousin to contribution.

Sometimes you can get a good sense of the meaning of a word by looking at its etymology. "Generosity" comes from *genere*, the source word in Latin, which means to beget, produce, create, cause to exist, bring to life. Being generous in a marriage is an ongoing effort that will allow and encourage a marriage to thrive. It *begets*, or *produces*, happiness.

It doesn't take a rocket scientist to understand that generosity and appreciation of the other spouse's efforts are crucial to a happy marriage and increased marital satisfaction. But scientists, being scientists, had to find proof for this concept.

As it turns out, there are studies on this. In one, "generosity" was defined as "small acts of kindness, displays of respect and affection" and "a willingness to forgive one's spouse his or her faults and failings." The study found that generosity was positively correlated with marital satisfaction, and if not present, the lack resulted in marital conflict and ruminations of divorce. Not too surprising.

Other research studies concluded that generous behavior communicated a desire to "invest in" the relationship and thereby could lead to its success and continuance. The receiver of generosity has an increased sense that their expectations for the relationships are met. This increases marital satisfaction and stability.

If giving and receiving are rated at roughly equal levels, partners in the relationship will report that they are happy in their marriage. This concept seems analogous to the concept of contribution to marriage, because contribution is also a gift of generosity. When contribution of spouses in a marriage is in balance, the marriage generally works.

This finding directly relates to prenuptial agreements.

The driving purpose behind most prenups is to identify resources and assets that will be held separately from the other spouse and put beyond their reach. Certainly, this is appropriate for some marriages. But, in its typical form, a prenup is the opposite of generosity. That's why prenups, what's in them, and the process of negotiating and formulating them should be of critical concern to couples contemplating having one.

There are many ways to make a prenup more generous. One of them is to incorporate into the contract planned generosity to the less-moneyed spouse, thereby lightening that spouse's financial load.

If a couple is marrying, then both of their strengths should be valued by each other.

Why punish a future spouse because they have fewer assets or more debt? There's probably a justifiable reason for that future spouse's situation. And there are many other reasons the more-moneyed person feels happy with the attributes of the other. Otherwise, they wouldn't be marrying each other.

If there is debt, a good way to handle such a situation is considering paying off that spouse's debt as a joint project after the marriage. (See Chapter 6.) Sharing your good financial fortune, whether self-made or inherited, is a demonstration of generosity that can and should be structured within a prenup.

If you are on your second marriage, making sure your spouse is secure after your death, even if you have children from your prior marriage, is a demonstration of generosity that will surely contribute to the overall happiness of your marriage. Caring about what happens to your spouse at the end of a long marriage that ends in divorce is also a demonstration of generosity that can be embedded into a prenup. Generosity in a prenup (and in a marriage) is rewarded, as the studies show, by generous behavior from the other spouse. Generosity can take many forms when two people share a life together.

• • •

The discussion on generosity and contribution reminds me of an old joke I heard in my childhood that was going around in my parents' generation. It goes like this:

A boy was born with a hexagonal nut in his navel. It caused him much embarrassment as he grew up. He couldn't remove it no matter how hard he tried. Finally, after he became a young man, he traveled to a remote mountain in Tibet because he heard that there was a wise man there who might help him remove the hexagonal nut. After climbing up the mountain he was told to sit down. The wise man told him to remove the hexagonal nut in his navel. The young man began to unscrew it. He kept turning the hexagonal nut. It took many hours until, finally, the nut came off. Very excited, the young man stood up, and his butt fell off.

Why do I bring up this joke here? What possible relevance does the joke about the hexagonal nut in the navel have to do with prenuptial agreements?

Jokes, as we all know, often have an element of seriousness. At their core, they may not be funny at all. The "hexagonal-nut-in-the-navel" joke is no exception.

It teaches us that we may not know the reason for something, but if we monkey around with it, we can destroy something very essential and precious. Removing the "nut in the navel" in a prenup by creating terms regulating a marriage that are different than what has developed in our laws and culture may have serious repercussions to a marriage. You are monkeying around with the very basis (the "boilerplate," if you will) of what a marriage is. So, when you design a prenup, make sure that you have not disturbed the basic balance implied in marriage. Otherwise, when you stand up — well, now you know the rest of the joke.

In this chapter, I've described the importance of generosity in marriage, the problems prenups pose, and how nonfinancial contributions are very important to acknowledge and appreciate in a long-term successful marriage. In the other chapters of this book, you will find much detail on techniques to build generosity into a prenup and how to balance this with the understandable and legitimate goals of the more-moneyed spouse or parties beginning a second marriage.

In all prenups, a balance needs to be struck between providing fairness, marital protection, and security for both parties, and an economic structure that reflects the parties' contributions of their time, attention, and work toward the success of the marriage. In other words, you *can* construct a thoughtful, caring and balanced prenup.

CHAPTER 6:

PAYING OFF YOUR FIANCÉ'S DEBTS

By and large, prenups contain knee-jerk provisions about how to deal with a future spouse's prior debts. They almost invariably state that each party shall be responsible for their own debts incurred before the marriage. On the face of it, that seems to make sense, right? But does it, really?

Part of the reason for that provision is the fear that the other spouse may become legally responsible for their fiancé's premarital debts. In fact, this concern is often the major precipitating factor for people in considering getting a prenup before marriage. Part of it, also, seems to be a moral judgment that the person who incurred the debt should be responsible for paying it.

Lots of financial advisors recommend prenups as protection against liability for a spouse's premarital debts. But is that accurate? And is it fair? And if you put this provision in the prenup, besides it being unfair (see discussion below), it signals distrust and lack of respect for the new spouse. Is that a message you really want to send (or receive)?

The general rule in all states is that *premarital* debt incurred by a spouse is that spouse's responsibility alone. (As for debts incurred after marriage, that's a different story. Some separate postmarital debts may be considered jointly owed, some not.)

As for separate premarital debts, in most states the debts of one spouse cannot be collected using assets owned by the other spouse. But a problem can occur when a couple buys joint property after their marriage. A debt collector can attempt to collect the separate debt owed by one spouse by attaching that spouse's interest in jointly held property. This would generally be deemed to be half the value of the joint property. Technically, the creditor cannot take the nondebtor spouse's interest in that property.

Trying to get half the value of jointly held property is difficult for a creditor. They would be forced to go through a full-fledged legal process. But even if the creditor were to prevail in that process, half of a joint interest (say, in a house) might have little saleable value. As a result, a creditor would not be inclined to exercise this option.

In a situation where there is significant premarital debt, it would be prudent to think about the possibility of collection against the debtor spouse's share when thinking about buying property *jointly*. The best strategy is to pay off the debt shortly after the marriage, if possible.

There are many solid reasons for paying off premarital debt when a couple marries, aside from freedom to own joint property without risk. The freedom from creditors of jointly owned property, however, is significant. For most couples, owning joint property that's marital is an important positive component of their marriage. It increases marital connection and satisfaction. So not being able to have joint assets because of a spouse's prior debts can be a significant setback to starting a marriage with solid financial, as well as emotional, underpinnings.

When a couple comes to me for mediation, and one has assets and wealth and the other has debt, perhaps even negative net wealth, I call it a "mixed marriage." I sometimes share my "mixed marriage" concept with the couple. I assure them that there's nothing wrong with that, and it's very common among marriages, especially in marriages with prenups. (It's often the underlying reason for the prenup.) It's just something to acknowledge and be aware of. There should be no value judgment.

People from different backgrounds, cultures, and economic situations often get together. The many people who are in "mixed marriages" can definitely work out their differences with understanding and respect. For many, the differences, if reconciled over a long marriage, bring richness to the marriage. Married people help each other with their different strengths and attributes.

But prenups tend to value money over most other things. That's understandable because that's what prenups are about: money. When you think of it, the less-moneyed spouse may bring many things to the table that the other spouse may not. There is the "standing on your own two feet" without parental help situation that increases advantageous qualities. People who have had to make it on their own generally possess resourcefulness and resilience. Often people from generational wealth need these qualities in a partner. A financially struggling future spouse may know things and have capabilities that their future spouse may not.

Often a person from a working-class or middle-class family comes to a marriage with significant student loan debt. The debt was incurred to finance their college and perhaps graduate school education. In the end, though, the student loan debt will likely benefit the marriage, because it prepared the spouse for more highly paid (and satisfying) work. Even if the spouse does not use the education for employment gains, it has still contributed to their personal growth, assuming you believe in the value of education.

Another factor to consider is why does one future spouse have student loans and the other does not? Usually, the answer is that the more-moneyed spouse's parents were able to help their son or daughter pay for their educational expenses. The working-class or middle-class parents did not have that level of extra income to be able to help their child with these expenses. College and graduate school are very costly.

Very few families have the discretionary income to pay for them in their entirety.

So, getting back to that prenup provision that says each spouse is responsible for their premarital debt; is it fair to penalize the future spouse who was not raised in an upper middle-class family or a family with wealth? Why should the child of family wealth be the sole beneficiary of the economic differences in their marriage?

Another issue is, where will the less-moneyed spouse find the money to pay off their student loans? Presumably it will come from their own earnings. But that means they will contribute less money toward the living expenses of the marital enterprise. It's really a zero-sum game. That's the flawed logic about saying that the spouse with student loans must pay off their own debt. The money must come from *somewhere*. So why not say in the prenup that the couple will pool all earned income and pay the student loans with that pooled income?

Doesn't it make sense for the couple to view the student loan debt as a household debt, similar to a mortgage? If there is great wealth on the part of one spouse, why not pay off the debt at the time of the marriage and treat it essentially as a wedding gift? Alternatively, a plan can be made to pay off the loan over, say, a period of five years. If there's a divorce before that time expires, the remaining obligation could be the responsibility of the person that incurred the debt.

A commitment to help one's spouse relieve a financial burden is a strong gesture of love, commitment, and generosity. A plan to pay off student (or other) debts signifies a deeper level of commitment and love than a wedding ring with a large diamond. Also, it's good for married couples to start off with a clean financial slate, if possible. One party shouldn't be burdened by something that's easily alleviated by the other party.

When both spouses commit to paying off the debt together, it can also help to cement a marriage. It means they really care about each other. But in most prenups, you'll find the knee-jerk term that premarital debt is the responsibility of the spouse whose debt it is. So, when you see that term in the first draft, think about it. Is that really what you want? Is that the message you want your less-moneyed fiancé to see? And it may put into question your choice of an attorney if that term had not been fully discussed with you.

Generosity can and should be alive and well even *within* a prenup, but only if the parties (guided by their attorneys) work together to ensure it is. That's how you can and should start to construct a generous prenup.

CHAPTER 7:

GENDER-BASED PROBLEMS IN PRENUPS

I often see my less-moneyed prenup clients acting from and making decisions that are driven by gendered cultural norms. If the less-moneyed spouse is a man, he will say he doesn't want anything to do with money he hasn't earned. He wants to appear strong, even though his salary is dwarfed by his future spouse's income or overall wealth. If the future wife's wealth was earned by her father, he is especially leery about having anything to do with that wealth. He doesn't want to appear weak to her father.

If the less-moneyed spouse is a woman, she often expresses her discomfort of possibly being seen as a gold digger. This happens despite her marrying because she loves the person who will be her husband — not to "get" his money. Oftentimes her fiancé's money or family wealth is actually regarded as a burden to a couple finding a happy path forward together.

The problems raised by these concerns are real. They cause people to act against their own best interests. They often ask for less than what they are rightfully entitled to when they are getting married with a prenuptial agreement.

That's why a future husband or future wife may voluntarily renounce the earnings or wealth of the more-moneyed partner before the marriage. I hear this all the time, both from male and female clients.

They may choose to disclaim their financial marital rights even if their decision could later leave them in a difficult position.

The male partner may say, "I don't need her money. I can make it on my own."

He has been taught that he is the one who makes the money in the family. To put it in cultural terms, the man is supposed to "bring home the bacon." To rely on her money (or her family's money) would be embarrassing to him and could certainly be a romance-killer. In fact, in this culture, when a man relies on a female spouse's money or earnings, it generally puts a damper on the romance. (The opposite effect, interestingly, is generally not true.)

The male partner has been taught to be in control and to be capable — in short, to "be a man." She is attracted to him because of these attributes. Her money, earnings, or financial success disrupt these mutual expectations. To nip this problem in the bud, he's willing to sign a restrictive prenup. He will usually sign almost anything to resolve this issue — no matter how restrictive the prenup may be. He may be too embarrassed even to negotiate the first terms sent over by the future wife's attorney. I have heard horror stories about the results of this fact pattern for the man when a divorce occurs, sometimes as long as 30 years later. These men often have insufficient marital funds to share in the end, due to the terms they agreed to many years before.

Situations change during a long marriage. It's unfair for a man to end up after 30-plus years with nothing to show for his work after having contributed all his earnings to the marriage. Maybe it seemed okay to him when he got married at age 30, but now that he's 60 or older and finds himself amid a divorce, this outcome doesn't seem fair (and is not fair) — and he's understandably worried about his future. Because of the prenup, he will be left with few assets and little income with which to retire. He wishes he hadn't signed that prenup and feels like he was a fool. He's right. He was foolish to sign it.

On the other side of the gender divide, I often represent women who are in the process of marrying very prosperous men. This is not surprising, because even in this era of employment advances for women, the data show that women still earn less than men on average, even for the same jobs. There are many reasons for this, and some relate to the primary interests many women have in family and other nonmonetary activities, so that careers may take second place for them.

Men generally do not have a problem marrying and supporting women who have less lucrative career paths than they do. I've seen men enter into second marriages without prenups, even if they're still paying alimony from their first marriages that ended in divorce, and even when their new wives are not actively engaged in the job market.

Sometimes it is even the less-moneyed woman who is the one who *initiates* the discussions about having prenups. They may have been dating and/or cohabiting with their male partners for a long time. They insist that they love them for who they are, not for their money, and want to prove their *bona fides* by willingly entering into a prenup. Often the terms of the prenups they are about to sign will make things worse for them than if they married someone without money but *without* a prenup. At least in that situation there could be a chance for significant marital property buildup during the marriage.

At many points during these negotiations, the woman will state that she doesn't want to be seen as a gold digger. At these moments, she might back away from terms that would benefit her and that are quite reasonable, even in a prenup. She is embarrassed by being the recipient of benevolence. She has always been financially independent and wants to remain so. Sometimes being married requires a change of mind-set, because mutual generosity is so important to its well-being.

Remember, prenups change the state law financial rules of marriage, generally to the detriment of the less-moneyed spouse. Both a male and a female spouse-to-be, who is trying to eliminate the perception (perhaps self-imposed) that they are a gold digger by signing a restrictive prenup, is putting themselves in a financially precarious situation.

When you marry with a prenup, you are substituting state laws with your own laws. Let's see how the law would treat someone who dedicated all their earnings to family expenses while their spouse possessed a good deal of family wealth.

There is ample case law already addressing this type of situation to cover people who *didn't* sign prenups. Generally, in these cases, the facts are these: The man provided all his earnings to support the family. The couple's mutual expectation was that the wife's family wealth (inherited, in trusts, and/or gifted during marriage) would provide for both their retirements. The divorce interfered with those expectations. A variation of this is that they have engaged in livelihoods that, while socially important (such as teaching), are not very remunerative.

The legal doctrine underlying this situation is termed "promissory estoppel." It occurs when someone makes a promise and another person reasonably relies on the promise, changes his or her position, and suffers a financial loss by relying on that promise. The person who made the promise is legally "estopped" by a failure to stand by it hence, "promissory estoppel."

To receive a promissory estoppel award for damages (unless voluntarily given by the promisor), one must file a lawsuit. In the case of divorce and the corresponding compensation for leaving the job market to have a family, the lawsuit is the divorce action. Divorce law essentially evaluates the loss when alimony and property division are determined.

In a case like this, the promise that was relied upon was that the family wealth would be shared during retirement and would be available to supplement the livelihood of the couple if they chose to be employed at less remunerative work during the marriage.

Where there is a divorce with no prenup (and if it's the wife who is the party with family wealth), she often insists in the divorce action that this wealth should not be shared with her husband but instead remain within the bloodlines. In these cases, courts will generally try to build equity into the situation by giving the husband some of the wife's inherited or gifted assets or, more often, a disproportionate share of the marital assets, in order to secure his financial future.

But if the couple had signed a prenup, the husband would have waived this equitable right, and the prenup would likely be enforceable, leaving him in the lurch after working all those years and supporting his family. (In case you're wondering — as I was — the word "lurch" alludes to a 16th century French dice game *lourche*, where to incur a *lourche* meant to be far behind the other players. It certainly fits this situation.)

There is a lot of media hype these days directed toward millennial women, encouraging them to lead separate and independent financial lives from that of their spouses or partners. An offshoot of this attitude is the flood of advice telling them to get prenups before they marry. Young millennial women are often willing to sign away their marital rights because they believe they should be forever financially independent from their spouse. They believe themselves to be putting forward a feminist vision of marriage.

These situations can, and often do, end up very badly.

At the beginning of a marriage, both parties to the prenup might be working and earning a living, but things may change during a marriage. Working roles might change. A spouse may decide to put their career on hold to provide more family care. Or by mutual decision, even if there are no children of the marriage, one spouse becomes the primary homemaker. Another problem this situation raises is that the more that spouses lead separate lives and the less financial connection there is between them, the weaker the marriage might grow over time.

For these reasons, every term in your prenup should be carefully thought out. Be very aware of what you are relinquishing in a prenup. Constructing prenup terms in a vacuum, without understanding what laws would apply if you didn't have a prenup, is not beneficial. You also should have a clear understanding of the reasons underlying the laws that you are waiving. It is vital for you to envision what problems might arise in the future if you forgo the laws pertaining to marriage at the time you're negotiating a prenup.

Be informed. Be an advocate for reasonable financial protections in a marriage. Whether you are a man or a woman, don't be a shrinking violet.

CHAPTER 8:

THE HOARDING AND CONTROL PROBLEM IN PRENUPS

As you have seen, generosity, contribution, and creating finan-cial security is crucial to the health and success of a marriage. Not realizing the negative consequences, many people (espe-cially young people) may sign prenups that distort these values and put negative pressure on their unions before they marry.

Two problems that may play out in marriages when there's a pre-nup are hoarding behavior and control issues.

All prenuptial agreements set up a distinction between "separate property" and "marital property." (The latter is termed "community property" in some states). This has a direct effect on the behavior of the spouse owning the separate property, and on the sensitivities of the non-owning spouse.

Hoarding behavior can occur when separate assets are established. There is a natural tendency for a spouse who maintains separate prop-erty to work to increase and preserve it. They may spend a lot of time and energy focusing on and acting in favor of those assets, sometimes to the detriment of building up marital assets.

Knowing that their spouse cares so much about their separate property can have a negative effect on the other spouse, resulting in bad feelings. If the prenup isn't a generous one and when a spouse spends much of their time on maximizing the results of their investment of separate assets, this is especially stinging.

This distinction between "separate" and "marital" property is bound to affect the undercurrents of the marriage, unless both parties are similarly situated in terms of assets and income.

What happens when the marital funds are inadequate to take a financial step that the couple wishes to take together? The less-moneyed spouse will wonder why a contribution of separate assets or income can't be available to make that financial step happen.

Most prenups trace or track contributions of separate property into joint property and, upon a dissolution of the marriage, require that the separate property be returned to the spouse whose contribution it was. Usually, the prenup terms state that the separate property contribution will share proportionately in any upside gain. This can make the marital relationship feel more like a financial, nonmarital partnership which can have a negative emotional impact on both spouses.

If a prenup (in a first-marriage situation) has the monolithic rule that premarital separate property as well as proceeds and gains from that property be kept as separate property, that person will have a natural tendency to remain keenly aware of it and try to maximize it. It's human nature. I call it "hoarding behavior," because it's akin to those who have a house piled up with newspapers, empty food containers, and a zillion cats. Financial hoarding resulting from prenup terms might be more socially acceptable (and sanitary), but the similarities are there.

Here's a scenario that comes up often:

One spouse has a separate checking account funded with separate property. That spouse has $100 in cash from that account. They go to the supermarket to do some food shopping for the family. That person is bound to think of that as "separate property" cash in their pocket, and will ask themselves, "Should I use it for the purchase?" It's likely that the family credit card will be taken out and used instead.

This may be a petty example, but it's real. The existence of prenups floods the marriage with thoughts about what's separate and what's marital. And it retriggers memories of the prenup and the prenup negotiations (which may have been unpleasant). It's how the hoarding issue really can infect a marriage on a daily basis.

The issue also arises when one of the spouses is engaged in an active business. Most prenups say that compensation for services, such as salary, stock options, and retirement savings, are deemed marital and are shared. But what if the money drawn by the spouse from the business consists of salary plus *profits*? What if the business *profits* under that prenup are *not* shared? The spouse who is the business owner may decide to keep their salary at a very low level that may in fact be dwarfed by the business's profits.

A variation is when the business itself is categorized as separate property. What if the business appreciates greatly in value during the marriage due to that spouse's efforts and talents? That is not going to feel good to the other spouse.

Hoarding behavior set in motion by prenups ends up being almost like an extramarital affair. People spend time thinking about their separate assets and acting in pursuit of protecting and growing them. This behavior is bound to make the other spouse feel neglected and unloved. Perhaps the marriage wouldn't have failed if there had been no prenup, or if the prenup terms had a more nuanced treatment dealing with the *efforts* of both spouses, not just their financial contributions.

Another issue that my prenup clients raise is that they feel uncomfortable having to keep track of separate property and shared property. These calculations can become very complex, sometimes causing the frequent participation of a CPA or tax preparer to perform them.

Because the couple needs to think about separate versus marital property, it may cause them to have flashbacks to the misery they experienced during the prenup negotiations. This could happen regularly, indeed every time they need to track separate property.

Relative control over decisions affecting the marriage is another issue that can lead to marital discontent. Prenups have the potential to exacerbate control imbalances. "Control" and "acknowledgment" (the latter a close cousin to "contribution") are often the main issues challenging marriages. In marriage, control needs to be shared. Otherwise, a spouse feels stuck, unheard, and powerless. Spouses need to feel that their efforts and input are acknowledged and appreciated. A spouse's input into financial issues is an important component of most marriages.

However, the terms of typical prenups often disrupt the natural flow of control and acknowledgment.

The first instance of control in the context of a prenup is when a future spouse says to their partner, "We need to have a prenup before we get married." The implication of this is that there will be no marriage unless this demand is met. I've discussed that issue in Chapter 3. When a person has invested years into a relationship, this is not really a choice.

There are particular provisions in prenups that tend to raise the control issue. For instance, it was customary in the past, and in some cases even now, that many attorneys insist that estate-planning provisions *not* be put in a prenup. They claim that spouses can do that by drawing up estate plans after they get married. The problem with that concept is that the structure of the estate plan is in the total control of *one* party. Always.

There is no law stating that someone cannot change the provisions of their estate plan the day before, even minutes before, they die. Who they name as their beneficiaries is totally within their purview. A pre-nup can specifically address a spouse's rights regarding being desig-nated as a beneficiary in a will or another asset, such as a retirement account. A prenup can make sure there is a "floor" inheritance require-ment. Without this protection, there is the potential for a devastating impact on a spouse. Knowing that their spouse can control this critical element of their financial well-being, may challenge a spouse's ability to advocate for themselves in the marriage. (See Chapter 9.)

Many spouses feel guilty if they earn less money than their part-ner. As a result, they may cede financial control to that other party. A spouse that is the higher earner may feel that all financial decisions should be made by them. Or they may both believe that the party who earns more is entitled to make all or most financial decisions.

This plays out in many ways in a marriage. I have seen a home-maker spouse have to move from the city or town they've lived in for years because the other spouse wants to move, even after retirement. The rationale is that the higher earner (the breadwinner of the family) gets to choose where the couple should live because that person made the money. On the other hand, I've seen couples stay in their home years after it makes sense to move when a spouse who is failing and can no longer stay safely in their home insists on staying there. A spouse who controls the purse strings may exert overbearing influence on such decisions.

And here's another situation that existed for generations: It's brutal, but it's real. If a party to a marriage has no financial control and does not have the wherewithal to end the marriage and find other living arrangements, that person is then "controlled" by the spouse who con-trols the money. This, of course, had been the plight of married women for ages. But it still exists for many people today. Because prenups over-ride divorce law, they can put spouses in an unprotected situation if one wants to end the relationship and move out. That's why loving partners should give each other a "good deal" in a prenup, even if the marriage ends in divorce, and not just give benefits and security if the marriage ends in death.

When spousal support is waived in a prenup, it will cause a lessening of options for a dependent spouse. To me, the provisions in a prenup relating to divorce are important protections for a spouse's freedom to be able to choose whether they want to stay in the marriage. Everyone hopes and intends that a marriage will last a lifetime, but sometimes marriages don't. And there need to be reasonable provisions included in the prenup to handle the situation when a marriage ends in divorce. Otherwise, a hurtful control issue is imbedded in the prenup.

Having joint financial accounts that are controlled by both parties helps maintain the dependent spouse's freedom to choose whether to stay in the marriage. Making sure joint property grows to a reasonable point in the marriage (depending on the circumstances) so that a spouse can choose whether to stay in the marriage is healthy. Having a mechanism for separate property to eventually become marital property in appropriate circumstances removes the control from being in only one spouse's hands. (See information about ways to vest separate property into marital property in Chapter 19.)

Let's say Michael and Joan entered a prenup. The prenup says that Joan (the more-moneyed spouse) can share her separate property with Michael as she sees fit during the marriage. So, yes, she can decide to freely contribute separate property to the marital estate and make that property marital. That is usually in all prenups. But in this type of prenup, one party has control over whether to contribute their property to the marital estate or keep it as separate property. And if Joan chooses not to share it, Michael may start to feel the sting of her decision. He starts to feel unloved. That's how a marriage can be disrupted when major financial decisions are made by just one of the spouses. It is another example of how destabilizing a prenup can be.

Another provision in a prenup that can have a negative effect on the marriage is the presumption that any separate property that's added to marital property maintains its separate character. This is a reflexive provision contained in most prenups. A better presumption in a prenup would be that if Joan puts money or property into joint ownership, that property is now marital property to be shared in the marriage, and her contribution will lose its character as separate property. (Most prenups have the *opposite* presumption — that separate money added to marital property remains separate, and is fully tracked as separate.)

Having separate property contributions to the marital estate presumptively become marital is a healthy provision to put in a prenup. It sets up an environment of generosity and caring. It has a positive psychological effect. It allows and encourages the more-moneyed spouse to be generous during the marriage. Joan still has control of what she wishes to share from her separate property, but the gifting presumption is written into the prenup. Generosity will become the blueprint for the marriage.

CHAPTER 9:

THE DANGER OF LEAVING OUT AN INHERITANCE REQUIREMENT

I t's well known nowadays that *everyone* who is getting married in this country has already signed up for a prenup. When you marry, you become subject to a comprehensive system of state laws pertaining to the economic rights and obligations of married people when you divorce.

There are many state laws that address — and are intended to protect — property rights upon the death of one of the spouses in a marriage. The moment you marry, these laws (whatever they are in your state) apply in full force. That's why it's very important to think about what happens if these rights are waived or not addressed in a prenup.

A common practice of attorneys drafting prenups is leaving out any discussion pertaining to the inheritance rights spouses have from each other. They intentionally omit what would occur when one of the spouses dies during the course of a marriage. The good news is more and more attorneys *are* including an inheritance clause these days. However, the practice of not addressing this important issue in a prenup still persists.

The intention to leave out inheritance rights most likely originates from the more-moneyed spouse's attorney, who, traditionally, wants all financial control retained for their client. They say (and convince their clients) that the inheritance issues should be addressed solely through their estate plans executed *after* the marriage. To me, leaving the issue of inheritance completely open is alarming on many levels, especially for the less-moneyed spouse.

Estate plans can be changed, often abruptly, as in the days, hours or even minutes before someone dies. This can leave a spouse who has been in a long-term marriage in a precarious financial situation. It also, depending on the specific facts, may be patently unfair. When you sign a prenup, the terms almost invariably take away spousal protections to inherit under state law. This is why it's so dangerous to leave this issue "open" in a prenup. There is absolutely no recourse for a disinherited spouse, because by entering into a prenup, the state laws that safeguard a disinherited spouse have been waived.

When you include terms in a prenup relating to inheritance, this part of the prenup is essentially a "contract to make a will," valid in virtually all states. This commitment is a contractual debt against a spouse's estate. However, the contractual agreement imbedded in the prenup should be followed up with a fully executed estate plan. This protects the spouses, because collection actions against third parties if someone dies without the required estate plan are very challenging. (See below.)

Also, one shouldn't forget to address nonprobate assets, such as retirement accounts, life insurance, annuities, and the like. The decisions about who will receive the distributions from these assets at death can be set in a prenup. Again, this needs to be followed up by making sure the applicable beneficiary designation forms on file with the financial institutions accurately reflect what is in the signed prenuptial agreement.

There may be several reasons why a person might disinherit their spouse without the spouse even knowing about it. Sometimes a spouse might be engaged in a relationship outside of the marriage at the end of their life. Or, prior to their death, a spouse may become eccentric or slightly senile (in a way that doesn't rise to the level of legal incompetence), or paranoid, or angry. A spouse may be unhappy about the health of the marriage right before their expected (or unexpected) death. Or the spouse may decide to leave their entire estate to their children from their first marriage, and the other spouse may never know about it until it's too late.

What follows is a brief discussion of state law inheritance rights that are waived in most prenups, followed by information on basic estate planning and options for people to consider when they draft inheritance provisions in their prenups. Then there will be a description of techniques to use in estate planning in prenups that can help regulate and determine estate provisions, including situations where there are children from previous marriages. Finally, I'll talk about the rights and remedies a surviving spouse has when the estate plan of the decedent violates the obligations that spouse made in the prenup and why it's important to actually create and execute the estate plan in accordance with the commitment made in the prenup.

• • •

Widows and widowers have rights to inherit in all states, even if there is no last will. When there is no last will, an estate is nonetheless administered as an *intestate* estate. Estates where there is a valid last will and testament are termed *testate* estates. Either way, the person administering the estate (called executor, personal representative, or administrator) controls the assets that the deceased spouse left titled in their name. These might be bank accounts, real estate, cars, stocks, securities accounts, and the like. The property in the decedent's name is termed *probate* property.

Probate property goes through the last will — if there is one — to the beneficiaries named in the will. If there is no last will, then the rules of intestacy apply. These state laws name the class of beneficiaries and will determine who will receive the deceased person's assets and the proportions in which they will be distributed. The right of a surviving spouse to an intestate estate varies from state to state. It is not necessarily 100 percent of the total probate estate. In many states and situations (e.g., if there are children of the marriage or prior marriages), it may be less than 100 percent, and is often set at 50 percent. This right to inherit via intestacy is almost always waived in a prenup.

Another protection provided to spouses under the laws of most states (a right that is routinely waived in prenups) is a spousal election to "take against the will" or "take a forced share." It's a law that protects surviving spouses who have been disinherited by the deceased spouse, or who are not satisfied with what they received through that spouse's last will and testament.

Taking against the will involves a court proceeding in which the widow or widower elects to take a statutory amount instead of what was (or what was not) left to that spouse under the will. What is received by that spouse is usually either a portion of the probate estate outright (usually one-half or one-third) or the interest generated by that share during the surviving spouse's life. Some states have adopted a more nuanced law relating to this right, a law that considers the length of the marriage, property transferred to the surviving spouse by other means (such as survivorship), and other factors. The exercise of this right is almost always waived in a prenup.

In addition to probate property, there are also other important types of property that are distributed by beneficiary designation rather than through a will. These include life insurance proceeds, annuities, retirement plans and accounts, and beneficial interests in trusts. Another common type of property consists of assets titled in joint names with survivorship features, which automatically go to the surviving joint owner. All these types of ownership and interests are termed *nonprobate property*. These nonprobate interests are very important when someone dies, and they often far outstrip the probate assets in value. They can also be changed easily by a spouse shortly before their death.

Another type of nonprobate property, often ignored or forgotten, can have unintended consequences upon one's death. These are bank and securities accounts that have been titled as "payable on death" (POD) or "transfer on death" (TOD). These accounts will go directly to the beneficiary named and will not go through the will. A surviving spouse will have no rights to this property under intestacy (or testacy) if they are not named in the POD or TOD designation. In addition, they will not be able to access the other spousal protection, "taking against" the will.

It is important when sharing financial information for a prenup that property titles and beneficiary designations for all these types of assets be reviewed carefully. Who are the beneficiaries now? Who should they be after the marriage? To whom is the POD or TOD asset going to be paid after death (if anyone), or should they be redesignated as estate assets? Who are the joint owners of any jointly held property? Does either party have any beneficial interest in a third-party trust? If so, what are the terms of that beneficial interest? Is there any possibility for a new spouse to receive payments from the trust if one dies first at a time when the marriage is ongoing?

You can now see why, when embarking on a prenup, it's a good time to make sure the titling and beneficiaries of your assets are what you intend them to be. For instance, many people forget that they may have set up an account jointly with someone else, or that they have named someone else (other than their future spouse) as their beneficiary of retirement accounts or other nonprobate property. This "housekeeping" is very important. After you marry (or even before), you may wish to redesignate these accounts for your spouse. You don't want your surviving spouse to encounter a nasty surprise with a large account that you meant to leave to them but will go to someone else because you forgot to change the beneficiary designation.

So, if you get married, don't assume that your spouse will get all your assets when you die. This depends on the intestacy laws and forced-share laws in your state, as well as what's in your last will. It also depends on your current designation of beneficiaries of your nonprobate assets and the titling of all your other assets. As has been discussed, when formulating a prenup, it is important to consider both probate and nonprobate property when thinking about the distribution of your assets if the marriage is ongoing at the time of your death. This is an integral part of the planning for your financial future that you should do when formulating a prenup.

It's important for the inheritance terms to be set in the prenup. But as you shall see, it's also important to have an estate plan incorporating those terms prepared and formally executed after the marriage.

Here are some possibilities regarding dealing with inheritance from each other that people employ in their prenups. There can be a "floor" provision for estate planning. These "floor" amounts can be articulated as "at least 50 percent of my estate will go to my spouse," or "all of our marital property shall go to the surviving spouse, and at least 50 percent of my separate property." It is important to define "my estate" in the prenup precisely. Of course, the inheritance floor requirement will only apply if the couple remained married at the time of death.

There will be an interplay between separate property, marital property (called "community property" in some states), joint property with right of survivorship, and property going to a spouse by beneficiary designation when figuring out how a floor provision in a prenup will work. These are choices that couples can make during the planning stage by evaluation and mutual agreement that will become terms in the prenup.

If it's a first marriage with no children yet but may be in the future, or there are no children from previous marriages, the customary estate planning in the U.S. is to leave the entire estate to the surviving spouse. The thought behind this is that the surviving spouse will need to take care of the children of the marriage and have control of the financial resources. I often encourage people to say something like "at least 90 percent to my surviving spouse" in the prenup, just in case there might be other gifts a person might wish to make in their estate plan.

Another important factor to consider is whether there are other family members of one of the spouses (such as parents or siblings) who might be dependent upon and still need financial help after the death of that spouse. If the new couple and their family have the means, the prenup could include provisions for a trust to be incorporated into their estate plan that could provide financial support for that family member.

It's a good idea to have a provision in a prenup that gives the parties the ability (by mutual agreement) to change their estate plan as needed, which may include departing from the original floor provision. In many states, this will be done through a formal postnuptial agreement. Many states require this as a policy matter, because the laws of postnuptial agreements provide more protection to spouses who are in an ongoing marriage than prenuptial agreements. Thus, a formal postnuptial agreement that describes the change in estate plans may be required to ensure that the estate change is not being forced upon an unwilling spouse. (See Chapter 18.) In some states, a coordinated estate plan signed with the same formalities of a prenuptial agreement may be adequate if the new estate plan does not lessen the rights of either spouse. An attorney should be consulted when contemplating this change.

There are a number of reasons why a young couple might wish to consider a complex estate plan rather than just having simple wills. If there are children of the marriage, many people would like their spouses to control their assets upon the first of them to die but wish to have the assets go into a trust to support their children after the surviving spouse dies, until the children reach maturity. The default age of inheritance for children without a trust is eighteen, quite young for handling their inherited resources, especially if it entails a large sum. This concern may be addressed in a trust with creating a schedule of distribution to the children at specific ages, usually beginning in their 20s.

One should keep in mind the unified federal estate and gift tax that applies to estates over a certain level as well as state estate tax and inheritance laws. Navigating these laws to provide as much money as possible for the family as a whole after a death is a common estate-planning goal of a married couple. Techniques for setting up trusts such as QTIP and credit shelter trusts are important planning tools. For the very wealthy, estate plans with generation skipping tax (GST) trusts and irrevocable trusts are often used.

For second marriages, especially with children from a prior marriage, the planning needs to be more nuanced than marriages of relatively young people without children or only with children of that first marriage. For these second marriages, the financial security of each spouse needs to be looked at and planned for. How much of these resources will be needed to support the surviving spouse? Is there a possibility for providing for a deceased spouse's children with a portion of the couple's estate at the time of that parent's death without causing an insecure situation for their surviving spouse?

Setting up life estates in real property (especially in the marital home) can be very helpful in addressing a spouse's concerns pertaining to what their surviving spouse's living situation will be. A life estate in real property is a title-holding mechanism in which someone (often the surviving spouse) has a right to live in that property during their life. The concept is also used in QTIP trusts that benefit a surviving spouse during their lifetime. In a QTIP trust, what is remaining can be directed to the children. In a second marriage, it might be directed to the children of a prior marriage.

A prenuptial agreement is a contract, and whatever is contained in the agreement about inheritance or beneficiary designations establishes a debt on the estate of a deceased spouse. But if the estate plan described in the prenup is not actually executed, a spouse will need to take a court action to enforce the obligation. That's why (if the couple has decided to provide inheritance terms in their prenup) it is still important to take that next step and execute the estate plans that conform with the requirements of the prenup.

The court action to enforce the debt created by the terms of a prenuptial agreement against an estate's probate assets is complicated, expensive, and takes a long time to resolve. Court actions to enforce violations in designating nonprobate assets are even more complex and difficult.

The payor of the nonprobate funds (e.g., the life insurance or annuity company, administrator of the retirement plan) will not abide by a contractual provision in a prenup. They will distribute the proceeds to the named beneficiary. Then the nonbreaching surviving spouse will have to file a lawsuit against that third party recipient to try to recover the funds. A similar problem exists if the deceased spouse has provided for the surviving spouse by setting up a trust prior to their death but then changes the trust terms in violation of the terms of the prenup.

This is a difficult situation, and luckily, one that doesn't happen very often. Having a requirement in the prenup goes a long way to ensuring that any changes that diminish a spouse's rights are well delineated. Most prenups have a "bad actor" clause to reimburse attorney and court costs of a spouse who is the victim of a breach of contract. A prenup can also provide a term requiring prior notice of any changes in estate plans made by the spouses, plus sharing the content of any such changes before execution of the documents.

The fact that the prenup provides a template for inheritance is important. But as you can see, it is equally important that a couple actually prepares and executes those estate plans within a reasonable time after the marriage so that lawsuits won't be necessary.

CHAPTER 10:

CONSIDERATION IN PRENUPS

How should a couple that is getting married feel with the final product of their negotiation? The result should be that both parties are happy with the terms. Maybe "happy" is not the right word. Maybe the word "comfortable" is closer to it. But both future spouses should feel that the prenup terms are reasonable, that they are fair to each of them. Both should feel that the terms won't detrimentally affect their marriage.

As previously discussed, it's important to think about balance, and control issues between the spouses in a prenup. And if you care about each other, planning for reasonable financial security for the less-moneyed spouse is crucial. Mutual control, participation, and security are important in a marriage, whether or not there is a prenup. And remember that you are creating something you are both supposed to *agree* with. After all, it's a prenuptial *agreement*.

Remember that when you're negotiating it. Don't take your attorney's advice and start out with a no-holds-barred, harsh prenup that offers nothing to your future spouse. This is a terrible way to begin the process, and it could well end the engagement. (I've seen this happen many times.) Starting this way, even if the relationship proceeds, has scarring effects.

A prenuptial agreement should not be handled like a business arrangement. It's something else. The parties to the agreement are getting married, not going into business together. Bargaining with each other about which state rights should be lessened for one of them feels incongruous when two people love each other enough to get married.

I've often been asked by a more-moneyed future spouse how to raise the issue of a prenup with their intended. This is a tender and difficult situation. One way is to find out what the law is for marriages in your state and factual situation and think about a way you can offer more than what the state would provide. Then you could lead the process with an offer of generosity and could open the conversation that way. Look at the state laws about marriage together with your fiancé. (The internet is a good place to start.) How do they fit your situation? Do they work for both of you? Discuss them together. Remember, the whole point of a prenup is to *vary* state laws. When you start discussing how each of you may (or may not) wish to vary them, you might find that you already have a lot of areas of mutual agreement.

In typical prenup situations (e.g., significant family wealth, marriages with substantial prenuptial property, second marriages with children of the first marriage), you might find that your future spouse expected the discussion and is not at all surprised or offended when you bring it up. And do leave time before the wedding for these discussions. In fact, do not raise the issue after a wedding has been planned, and preferably raise it before the engagement. That's fair play.

This is where the mediation process can be very beneficial. A trained lawyer/mediator can facilitate discussions about the prenup and the various possibilities for its content. (In Chapters 20 and 21, I'll discuss the best methods for finding prenup mediators and prenup attorneys.) Many people also begin to see a marital counselor at this point, which can be quite helpful. Knowing that the angst you are experiencing is typical and common for people trying to negotiate a prenup is reassuring.

In my experience, once a fair and equitable prenup plan is developed, there are many plusses for the less-moneyed spouse. A prenup offers certainty of financial results that, if fair and equitable, give both parties security in going forward. In many respects, prenups increase the protections for the less-moneyed spouse than are present in state law. A good example of this is having an inheritance protection (if the marriage ends in death) in the prenup. Another is making sure there is marital property or community property developed during the marriage to adequately secure the less-moneyed spouse, even in cases where the other more-moneyed spouse doesn't need it, as in the case of early retirement of a successful entrepreneur.

There are other techniques that I'll describe in this book that can be used to reasonably meet the more-moneyed spouse's desire for protection and fairness but can also benefit the less-moneyed spouse. Having provisions in the prenup that will cause their beloved to smile rather than weep is a good thing. (See Chapter 19 to learn what these might be.)

The legal definition of a contract is that there must be mutual assent, consideration, and capacity to contract. We've just discussed how genuine "assent" can come about in the prenup context. The last requirement, capacity to contract, should be easy to meet for most people getting married. But what about consideration?

Normally, a contract needs to be supported by *consideration*. That means something of value needs to be exchanged between the parties to make it a binding contract. Another way to put it is that a promise is made, and someone gets paid for that promise when the work is completed. Here's an example: "I will plow your driveway, and you will pay me $50 for doing it." A trade for full value is being made. In a prenup, it could be something like, "If you waive alimony, I'll divide marital property 65/35 percent in your favor instead of 50/50 percent."

But for some reason, in prenups, the concept of consideration is missing. Treatises that develop uniform prenuptial agreement laws (which are often embedded in state statutes and case rulings) state that consideration is not necessary in a prenup. They say that the marriage *itself* is the consideration for the prenup.

I find the concept (not universally held) of not requiring legal consideration (other than the fact of the marriage) in a prenup troubling on many levels. It sounds to me like the more-moneyed spouse is getting paid twice.

The person is paid the first time by the willingness of the person they love and want to spend their life with to marry them. The mutual willingness to marry is consideration that has already been exchanged. (Maybe one spouse earns a lot of money, and the other has personality traits or physical beauty that make that person equally desirable as a spouse.) But then one person is asking the other to forgo additional rights — legal rights — to which they are entitled at the time of the marriage. Isn't that double payment? That's why a prenup should offer benefits to future spouses on *both* sides.

Taking away state law marital rights as a requirement to marry shows lack of "consideration" in the generic sense of the word. The lack of consideration causes a problem, because the person giving up rights often believes that they have been "had" or taken advantage of — not a good way to start a marriage. To really grasp what that means, let's look at the basic meaning of the word "consideration."

The word "consideration" has meanings and implications in addition to its technical use in contract law. It's derived from the word "consider," as in "to take into account," "to think," or "to propose."

The word "considerate" is a close cousin to that word. It's inextricably linked to the legal term "Consideration." The word's early meaning was "marked by deliberation," or the character of a "deliberate" or "prudent" person. But around 1700, it started meaning showing care or empathy toward another person.

Here are some of the meanings of "considerate" I found:

- Showing concern for the rights and feelings of others.
- Having regard for the needs of another.
- Aware of and respecting other people's feelings.
- Being respectful of others.
- Having regards for others.
- Being mindful of others.
- Characterized by consideration or regard for another's circumstances or feelings.
- Not heedless or unfeeling.
- Careful not to inconvenience or harm others.
- Paying attention to the wishes of another.
- Being kind.

Don't these sound like things that you and your fiancé should be manifesting in the months before your wedding (and afterward)?

Keep these meanings in mind as you go through the process of formulating and negotiating your prenup. Reclaiming that core meaning of consideration as being *considerate* is of utmost importance in finding a way to make both of you happy, or at least content about your prenup and the process. After all, one of the hallmarks of a good marriage is for spouses to be considerate of one another. That's why prenups are often so jarring to those embarking on a marriage. It's because they are often so inconsiderate.

So, when you create a prenup, make sure it's one filled with consideration for your future spouse.

CHAPTER 11:

TYPICAL BAD TERMS IN PRENUPS

When I review prenups for clients, I look for terms that raise "red flags" for me. Some of these terms, which I consider dangerous and distorting for first marriages, are totally acceptable and understandable in second and later-in-life marriages. So, most of the following comments relate to first marriages or early-in-life marriages, when marital sharing of assets and income are usually two of the most important factors in determining overall marital satisfaction and achieving marital success.

Some prenup drafts propose no sharing of earned income. This sets up an artificial division that is destabilizing in a first marriage. It puts the spouse who earns more than the other in control of how the couple's income will be shared.

Often couples have a disparity in their earnings. Some is due to their own interests. Some people are homebodies, or introverts. Some people like to be out in the world. Some people like competition. Some like nurturing and relationship-building. Differences like these can add to the strength and satisfaction of a marital bond.

Is the work of a public schoolteacher less valuable than the work of an investment advisor? One could say that the substantial income of the investment advisor enables the couple — as a unit — to contribute in their own unique ways to society. The remunerative work of one allows the other to work in the public sector as a teacher, for example, enriching the lives of a multitude of children for the betterment of all.

And when one of the spouses is a stay-at-home spouse — a homemaker and the primary caregiver during the day — the disparity in financial control (and income) can be even more pronounced. Without income sharing, the "contributions" of each spouse are not recognized and may not be truly appreciated. (I talked about "contribution" to marriage in Chapter 5.)

Then there's the issue of what's *included* in earned income. Is it just salary? Is it salary and bonuses? Does it include employee and employer contributions to retirement accounts? These are usually considered earned income because they are *deferred* earned income, and are benefits that accrue from employment. These items should be explicitly stated as being included in the definition of shared earned income.

There are also other employee benefits that may be accrued from the work outside the home. Some of these are stock options, restricted stock units (RSUs), phantom stock, stock appreciation rights (SARs), performance shares, and profit sharing. These types of rewards for employees are directly related to a person's activities in the workplace, and therefore they are part of their "contribution" to a marriage. A prenup should be specific about including these, and since there are always new forms of compensation, the term "and the like" should probably be added to the end of the list.

If one of the spouses is engaged in a business, there is the question of what compensation from the business will be shared in the marriage. Will it just be salary? Or will it include business profits? What if profits need to be put back into the business to make it survive and grow? And what happens to the increase in value of the business during the marriage? If the prenup just says that the business owner's "salary" will be shared (which I've seen in prenups), and most of the compensation is through "profits," this could result in an adverse situation for the other spouse. It would naturally lead to bad feelings and marital weakening. (See Chapter 14 for more information on businesses and prenups.)

Another issue to consider is whether income from separate property should be shared during the marriage. This is a personal issue that will need to be addressed in each case. There is no "one-size-fits-all" solution. Even if the final decision is that income generated from separate property remains separate, it's important to think about it together and discuss it. If you consider this concept, you could mutually decide that income from certain premarital assets will be shared and income from others not shared, or could be limited.

There are terms that I view as negative in prenups that involve the home the couple will live in.

Some marital residences are initially owned by one of the parties. Some prenups do not contemplate or make plans for eventual joint ownership of the marital home. Living in a jointly owned home is important for most people for many reasons, some of them having to do with the aspirational view of the marital partnership.

Also, a home, like children, is something that brings couples closer together. Having a stable home, even if it ends up being more expensive than renting (it usually is), has great importance for most people. It may not feel right for only one spouse (or that spouse's family trust) to own it. It means that the other non-owning spouse is the one that must move out if the marriage ends in divorce. Even if the marriage is ongoing, contemplating this harsh result may cause marital friction and annoyance.

I've often seen the following especially negative term in some prenups in a case where the parties are living in a house owned by only one spouse. The prenup may say that if the marriage ends in divorce, the non-owning spouse must vacate the house in 30 or 60 days. I've seen engagements break up because a home-owning spouse (at the advice of their attorney) included this provision in the first draft given to the other spouse. It can be an extremely cruel and insensitive provision to lay out in a prenup right before marriage.

If the home is owned by one of the spouses at the time of the marriage, it is a good idea to have a plan to create joint ownership over time, or to purchase a new home that's jointly owned. Having both spouses own a house is something that's important and stabilizing for most couples. It also increases the "skin in the game" for a marriage. Neither may want to move out. As a result, sometimes couples wait out periods of marital stress and often resolve their differences.

If family trusts are involved, the terms of the trusts need to be understood by both future spouses. Sometimes a couple might be living in a house owned by a family trust, so they will never have "their own" home. Also, there may be decisions to be made about other benefits and distributions coming out of the trusts and other issues to analyze relating to the trusts that will affect the marriage. Most attorneys for the more-moneyed spouse simply take family trusts off the table and don't want to enter into discussions about their impact on the couple and their future children. But the trusts are real, and the money coming out of them needs to be addressed and discussed as part of the prenup process. (See Chapter 13 for further discussion.)

Most prenups say that any time separate property is contributed by a spouse into marital property, the separate property contribution will be traced or tracked. These standard prenups state that when the property is sold, the separate property component will receive a percentage of the gain or loss in value relative to the original contribution. Perhaps the opposite presumption works better for a marriage — if separate property is added to marital property, it loses its characteristic as separate property. (A spouse can just decide not to contribute it.) Or if tracked, the return on the separate property is dollar for dollar, not a percentage of the property's gain in value. Otherwise, the marriage becomes more like a business deal, which may be detrimental to the couple's feeling of being married.

In many prenup situations, one of the spouses has earned and accumulated enough money not to ever have to work again. This could have occurred before normal retirement age, or if it's a gray prenup, it could happen when that future spouse has retired from working at the usual age. The other future spouse might very much still need to accumulate assets to secure their future. In a first marriage, normally this is done over time with marital savings and investment from pooled earnings. But what if it is a second marriage with a pronounced asset disparity?

Things might work out okay if the marriage ends in death, but what if the marriage ends in divorce? Such people also deserve to accumulate funds that appropriately secure their future. In these cases, some sort of "deemed" accumulation of marital assets (or transfer of separate assets to that spouse) needs to be worked out and imbedded in the prenup. When this is missing, the less-advantaged spouse could be in a very bad place if the marriage ends in divorce. And that spouse will be very aware of it. Good for the marriage? No, it isn't.

In Chapter 9 of this book, I discussed the importance of having an inheritance provision in a prenup. This requirement for a minimum or floor inheritance from each other is intentionally lacking in many (if not most) prenups. I explained in that chapter, why this lack of a commitment is not a good idea. Yes, the inheritance plan can be done after the marriage by formulating and signing estate-planning documents. But the prenup guarantees that it will happen, be put in place, and not changed by one spouse to the detriment of the other in a long marriage.

One of the most important features that is usually not included in most prenups (and in my opinion should be) is a robust Alternative Dispute Resolution (ADR) requirement. This comes into play if the couple can't come to an agreement if they divorce, notwithstanding the terms set forth in the prenup.

The pecking order is mediation followed by collaborative law. (In case you don't know what collaborative law is, you'll find a description in Chapter 20.) And if these methods don't work to resolve a dispute, the couple can use binding arbitration. Note that binding arbitration is not available for child support and custody. The courts always have ultimate jurisdiction of those issues involving children of the marriage.

The ADR requirement should also specifically apply to the heirs, executors, trustees, and administrators of a deceased spouse when resolving disputes with a surviving spouse in an intact marriage that ended in death. This will keep parties out of long, protracted and expensive court cases, and will give them peace of mind, especially when one of the spouses in a second marriage had experienced an aggressively litigated divorce in their prior marriage.

CHAPTER 12:

WHAT TO DO ABOUT PREMARITAL ASSETS AND INHERITANCES

P eople are getting married later in life these days. Many of my prenup clients are embarking on first marriages in their early 30s, and some are even older. They often have established careers before they marry. As a result, many of my prenup clients have accumulated significant assets prior to their marriage. In legal terms, these assets are called "premarital property." In most states, premarital property is considered the property of the person who accumulated the assets before the marriage, and these assets do not have to be shared with the new spouse.

For people considering prenuptial agreements, the primary concern is usually the situation where one future spouse has built up assets during their 20s and 30s, while the other has not. The person with the lower net wealth may have worked in the public sector. Or they may have substantial student loan debt that they are gradually paying off. Or they may not have prioritized financial success when choosing their career path.

The buildup of premarital assets by a future spouse can be significant. I have seen people in their late 30s who have accumulated $1 million or more in assets by the time they marry. And have done this without the help of family money and not working in particularly lucrative careers. Although this is unusual, it will lead the person who has accumulated the assets to wonder about the possible benefits of having a prenup.

This person, by their own hard work, by their forgoing luxuries, and through diligent saving and investing, wonders if they would be required to share — perhaps equally — the premarital assets accumulated at so much personal cost if there were to be a divorce. This is a reasonable concern that can be addressed in a prenup in many ways. Remember, in a prenup, you are "creating" your own laws — and these should help ensure certainty. They will serve as the template for the financial plan for the marriage. (But, of course, always keep generosity in mind.)

Some people marrying for the first time may have received substantial gifts from their parents (who might be still living). Some have already received inheritances from parents or grandparents when they embark on their first marriage. In these cases, the inheritances and gifts may represent a substantial portion of their premarital property.

The disparity in premarital wealth should not be a bone of contention. Instead, the couple needs to address the possible implications of the disparity. Addressing and discussing issues like this and not avoiding them is important in creating sound prenups.

But first, a little background on what "the law" says should happen to premarital property and inherited or gifted property if a couple gets divorced. That's the real underlying issue here. Will the person who has the premarital wealth get to keep it under state laws if the marriage goes south?

The presumption (the "black letter law") in virtually every state is that the property developed during a marriage is divided equally, even if one of the parties was the primary income earner and the other was focused on homemaking and childcare. Different rules generally apply to inherited property and premarital property.

The theory behind equal distribution of marital property is that each of the parties may have different roles in a marriage, but that marriage functions as a partnership, with each spouse's efforts deemed commensurate to the other's. Each of their efforts is termed "contribution" to the marriage and is generally legally found to be equal.

When making the asset division at divorce, some states look at *all* property, including property accumulated before the marriage as well as property received by gift or inheritance before or during the marriage. The law would then consider it all "marital property" subject to division. Usually what happens is that some or all of that premarital and gifted or inherited property may be taken out of the marital "pot." This would be under the applicable equitable doctrine based on the facts of a particular case. These considerations may result in sharing these assets (or some of them), especially in a long-term marriage, when not enough marital property has been developed to adequately secure each party.

In short marriages, premarital property and inherited property are generally not included as part of the marital property estate. In those cases, people usually "take back the marbles" they brought into the marriage. Sometimes adjustments are needed to put a spouse in a short-term marriage back on their feet.

Premarital property and inherited property may have been blended into "the fabric of the marriage" to support the marital enterprise. If so, this type of property (or some of it) might be more likely to be included as marital property.

What if an inheritance was expected and counted on by the couple during their marriage? What if this expectation was the basis for many important marital decisions? A couple may have made mutual decisions about how to earn their livelihoods during the marriage based on the expectation that they had present and future security based on family wealth. For instance, the spouses may have decided to work in nonprofits, or as artists or writers. They may not have saved for retirement, counting on an inheritance from the parents of one of the spouses to provide for them after they stopped working.

In that case (in some states), an inheritance may be divided between the spouses as marital property upon divorce, but not necessarily equally. It depends on the needs of the parties, as well as their ages. The court may be concerned in "gray" divorces of older spouses that each spouse is adequately protected for the future. At times, expectations of future inheritances may become relevant, as in the case of a 65-year-old divorcing couple, where one spouse will receive a huge inheritance from an aged parent soon after the divorce.

In summary, in some states, there is an aim to have an *equitable* distribution of all property if a marriage breaks up. Relying on state laws is intended to provide a fair result. This is actually the minority view.

In most states, there are laws that specifically protect and designate premarital property, and gifted and inherited property, as separate property. They also include any appreciation of that property and income flowing from it as being separate property. Some of these states I call "quasi-prenup" jurisdictions, because, except for the rule about premarital and inherited property as being separate property, marital property is divided by equitable distribution.

Other states have imported legal concepts from France and Spain rather than from England into their laws. They are the so-called "community property" states: Arizona, California, Idaho, Louisiana, New Mexico, Nevada, Texas, and Washington. The U.S. territory of Puerto Rico is also a community property jurisdiction. Alaska has adopted an "elective" community property system for residents. In that state, a resident can opt into community property treatment. These states have embraced the European cultural tradition that legacies coming from bloodlines should stay separate from marital efforts.

The basic principle of community property law is that the acquisition of property by labor by either spouse during the marriage is seen as a contribution to the marriage and therefore marital property. The presumption is that the relative value of the contribution made by each spouse is equal, no matter what form their contribution to the marriage takes. One party's labor can be in the workplace; the other party's labor can be at home.

In community property states, marital property is generally equally divided, without considering equitable factors. Title to property acquired during the marriage (that is, whose name the property is titled in) may not be relevant to its characterization. If an asset is deemed community property, it belongs to the community and is considered marital property, regardless of whose name is on the title.

Inherited property and gifted property (that is, property gifted by third parties, such as parents during their lifetimes) are considered separate property, not to be divided in a divorce. This rule also applies to premarital property.

The laws pertaining to income from separate property may be different in certain community property states. For example, in most of these states, income generated by separate property such as rents, dividends, or interest remains separate property during marriage. But in other states, income from separate property may become community property during the same marital period.

Here is an interesting issue to think about when planning for inheritances in a prenuptial agreement:

What happens if both parties expect to inherit from their parents, but the timing is likely to be different? One spouse's parents might be 10 years or older than the other spouse's. In addition, one never knows whether the expectancy of an inheritance may even come to pass, or if it will pass in a trust rather than outright. Asking a parent about their net worth when discussing your prenup can feel very awkward and intrusive. There probably are alternative ways to estimate their financial situation based on other information you may have.

Any time there is separate property in a first marriage, it has the potential to drive the spouses apart. So, if a couple wishes to share their inheritances, it might be a good idea to set the time for sharing when all four of their parents are no longer living. The couple may also opt to keep their inheritances separate. The prenup can state that if inherited money is used for family purposes (such as for the children's education), it is transformed into marital property.

If only one of the spouses has a substantial expectancy of inheritance, then a couple embarking on a prenup should decide what to do about it. You can choose to keep it separate. Or keep it separate, but have part of it vest into marital property over time. Other possibilities are having the income generated by the inheritance added to marital property, having any increase in value be deemed marital property, or both. Finally, a couple can decide to have the entire principal (the asset value) of the inherited property vest over time. Remember, we are talking about a prenup, so you can set your own rules.

What if the parents of one spouse regularly give their child lifetime gifts? One can view this as a "pre-inheritance" and follow the same rules as those set in the prenup for inheritances. Or a rule can be set in the prenup that says that gifts less than a certain dollar amount become marital at the outset, and gifts over that amount are treated in whatever way the couple decides to treat inheritance. You will need to set that dollar amount to something that feels comfortable for you, and probably increase it by the Consumer Price Index (CPI) so that the purchasing value of the target amount stays the same over time.

As I have pointed out, the existence of premarital property comes up often when discussing a prenup, even in first marriages. What to do about premarital property is especially important to evaluate when constructing a prenup because the nature of separate property's mere existence can cause conflict in a marriage if not properly addressed.

In a prenup, premarital property can be kept separate or can be shared over time. The specific rules should be imbedded in the prenup. The same approaches used for inheritances can apply to premarital property. (See above for the various possibilities.) The "snapshot" approach, providing that the value of the premarital property is fixed at the time of the marriage and that any gain or income derived from this property is deemed to be marital, seems fair to most people, and is easy to track. Or the couple can decide to vest all (or some) of the premarital property over time as the marriage manifests its strength and durability.

I frequently run across the following scenario regarding premarital property: Often it involves a first or second marriage, where a business owner has created and sold their business for a substantial sum. That person has no need to accumulate marital property, since they have secured their finances for the rest of their life. In fact, they no longer need to be employed to earn money at all.

However, they now wish to get married to someone with the more usual situation. That future spouse needs to accumulate marital property to secure their future, whether the marriage ends in divorce or death. They are entering into a marriage in which, legally and ironically, the only property deemed marital property will be the earnings of that less-moneyed spouse.

If you find yourself in this situation, you need to address it. The most common and logical way is to have the independently wealthy spouse transfer some of their premarital assets over time into the marital property pot. This can be done in many ways, using differing calculations, depending on the situation and the amount of money involved. The transfer can be an actual physical transfer (into a joint account), or "deemed," in other words, made as a bookkeeping entry. It can also be a combination of both actual and deemed.

If you care about someone, you shouldn't want to leave that person unprotected after a marriage of many years (even if it ends in divorce). The marriage might have failed because of the sting of not requiring you to protect your new spouse. Financially protecting the person you love shows you care, which is essential to enjoying a good and happy long-term marriage.

Most "stock" premarital agreements consist of the first draft sent by the attorney for the more-moneyed spouse. They almost always reflexively say that premarital property always remains separate property, unless the owner spouse decides to share it. But this does not have to be the case. Think about it. There are many decisions about premarital property that can be made in a prenup, and given some thought, can be made in an informed and kind manner.

The ramifications of having premarital or inherited property defined as separate are significant. You should be aware of several considerations when you make these choices. The discussion between you and your fiancé can be very awkward and difficult. Having these difficult conversations in the context of mediation with an informed mediator serving as facilitator can be extremely helpful. (See Chapter 21.)

Remember, in a prenup, you are making your own "law." But you also need to be familiar with the laws in your state pertaining to marriage and divorce. Consider your own views, concerns, the facts of your particular situation, your conception of what marriage is, and what you want your marriage to be. Then decide about how you want to treat your premarital and inherited assets. It's your choice.

CHAPTER 13:

PRENUPS FOR CHILDREN OF WEALTHY PARENTS

Having enough money is a good thing. A recent university study shows that when a person is in that middle range of income, one's day-to-day emotional well-being and satisfaction with life (one might call it "happiness") is the best and most ideal circumstance it can be. It's kind of a sweet spot. People suffer emotionally when their income is not sufficient to pay their bills and as a result, usually go into debt. It's a very unfortunate circumstance in which to live.

But people may also suffer when their income or wealth is much higher. Prime among them are the children of wealthy parents, whether the parents are "self-made" or have inherited the wealth from prior generations.

When a child of a wealthy parent gets married, there are many thorny issues to be addressed about the impending marriage. Most children of wealthy parents enter prenups at the behest of their parents, especially if the wealth is generated by a family business that is still ongoing.

This is not necessarily a bad thing. Like other financial factors leading people to have prenups, family wealth is something that needs to be looked at, analyzed, understood, and planned for as part of the overall marital plan. The issue should not be swept under the rug as "family money" or "money for our children and grandchildren" or "not my money." Remember, at its essence, a prenup is a financial plan for a marriage. So, when family wealth is why you're getting a prenup, the ramifications of this wealth over the long time period of a marriage needs to be openly discussed and planned for.

I have become aware through my clients' experience that having family wealth can be a mixed bag. It provides financial safety, security, and the ability to be able to enjoy things that cost money. But there are downsides, too. Great wealth usually creates great stress. It has been described to me as a burden. My clients report that they must be discreet about their family wealth when first meeting someone as they worry it might change how they are perceived. Sometimes the secret must be kept during the entire friendship. This can result in a sense of social isolation.

Children of wealth report a sense of guilt, since they didn't earn the money they are enjoying. And they almost invariably feel that their familial wealth has deeply affected their lives, causing them to constantly consider its ramifications. These future spouses are aware that they did not choose the family they were born into or the wealth that they benefit from. So family wealth, as it turns out, is a burden and an unchosen responsibility in many ways.

Part of growing up and developing as a person is accepting the hand you are dealt. A child of wealth must define and accomplish their own goals and interests. With family wealth, sometimes, the family's needs and goals are paramount and limit the children's choices. (Children of celebrities are also faced with these types of challenges and burdens that other people don't have to deal with.) Ultimately, we are all searching for the meaning of life, regardless of our wealth. People who have family wealth face the same quest. But with the additional complexities in their situations, it can be particularly challenging.

There's a very important factor in the cases where one spouse comes from a wealthy family and the other does not that should be taken into account. The nonmoneyed spouse usually takes on the role of supporting the other in living with the confusing and difficult issues raised by significant generational family wealth. This role is extremely important and should not be discounted. It's the type of support that the person whose family has the wealth cannot get anywhere else. At its essence, the nonwealthy spouse in marrying has not only accepted the benefits of wealth, but also shares the burdens.

Many times, the family of wealth has already put into place sophisticated estate-planning techniques that often involve irrevocable trusts. These trusts are structured as irrevocable because they address a particular element of estate tax law: the gain on any assets, once they are put into the trust, will no longer be part of the parents' taxable estate when the parents die. Since the highest marginal tax rate for estate taxes is currently 40 percent (after a very large exemption currently available), part of the reason these trusts are established is to minimize estate tax liability in the future.

Another reason for setting up irrevocable trusts is to pass assets from generation to generation through bloodlines. It's as if the hands of the dead ancestors are controlling future generations by conferring wealth on them. This is a problem, because now each generation may face the "struggle" of unearned wealth that the current new couple is facing.

Another purpose of setting up irrevocable trusts is to protect the trusts' assets and distributions from claims of a child-beneficiary's creditors. It is understood that one of creditors that the trust is trying to protect the trust beneficiary from is that person's soon-to-be ex-spouse. Trusts are also set up to protect the beneficiaries from their own financial missteps. To provide these protections, trusts almost always have a "spendthrift" clause in them.

Although the "thrift" in the word "spendthrift" may make you think of people who are very careful *about* money, a spendthrift refers to someone who does things such as bet their beneficiary interest in a trust in a poker game. It's a confusing term, because the "thrift" in the term derives from an obsolete meaning of the word, *prosperity* rather than *frugality*. So, it's actually a person who spends their prosperity (money) in an extravagant and irresponsible way.

The spendthrift clause in a trust goes something like this:

A beneficiary may not sell, pledge, or otherwise transfer any part of his or her interest in this Trust, and the Trustee shall not recognize any such transfer attempted. The interest of a beneficiary in this Trust shall not be subject to be taken by his or her creditors (other than the trustee in his or her capacity as trustee of this Trust) by any process whatsoever.

This not only protects the beneficiary's interest in the trust from their own improvident financial behavior, but seeks to protect the trust share from creditors, including an ex-spouse. The question of whether a spouse's claim on some of the assets of a trust in a divorce is valid, notwithstanding a spendthrift clause, is a question that is addressed in state laws and court cases in various ways.

It is clear, however, that once a beneficiary receives money from a trust, it may be subject to claims of spousal support and/or child support. To the extent that the money has purchased assets, depending on the state laws, those assets may be deemed property subject to division in a divorce. Sometimes claims are made against the trust itself, usually unsuccessfully. Prenups can provide alternative and enforceable terms for moneys coming out of a trust to a beneficiary, and terms to protect the trust *corpus* (its assets). But what the prenup's terms ought to be is something that should be thought about and addressed during the process of developing a prenup in a balanced way.

There are several factors that may come into play when analyzing the implications of irrevocable family trusts when it comes to divorces. Trusts that require a trustee to distribute principal at certain times (for example, all principal to be distributed to the beneficiary when the beneficiary reaches the age of 40) may be a factor into whether that expectancy will be considered when dividing marital property in a divorce.

Trusts also have various typical distribution treatments. Most asset protection trusts drafted by the advisors of wealthy parents are discretionary. In that type of trust, the trustee can decide when and how much of the trust funds to give a beneficiary. Typical language in a trust may allow for the trustee to have "complete and unfettered discretion" or "sole and uncontrolled discretion" in determining whether and to what extent a trust's income or principal should be distributed to a beneficiary. This type of trust is generally quite (but not always) protective in the case of a divorce.

Some trusts require that the trustee consider the "needs" or "comfort" of a beneficiary when making distributions. Some require the trustee to investigate other resources available to the beneficiary before making discretionary distributions and, in some cases, they are to disregard such other resources when making distributions.

In many trusts, the trustees are required to adopt the health, education, maintenance, and support (HEMS) standard when making distributions of income and principal to a beneficiary. Where trust distributions of income or principal are subject to the HEMS standard (or another specifically articulated standard), there is the chance that an ex-spouse with support rights may have an indirect right to trust assets since the beneficiary-spouse would have a right to compel payments from the trustee.

There may also be a group of beneficiaries of one trust fund, all of whom can receive discretionary distributions, which may be unequal and/or sporadic. This is called a "pot" trust. These trusts might have a trigger event (a beneficiary attaining a certain age, or the death of the person who created the trust), at which time what's left in the trust is divided among the group of beneficiaries. This provides some protection in divorces (at least prior to the trigger dates), because the amount that will eventually be distributed to the spouse-beneficiary is uncertain.

But having said that, discretionary trusts and HEMS trusts established by third parties (such as parents) and pot trusts can provide some protection to a divorcing beneficiary spouse in many states. This holds especially true if (as is customary) if the trustee is an "independent" trustee, one that is (supposedly) not controlled by the beneficiary.

Third-party irrevocable trusts (trusts set up by parents or grandparents) can have significant relevance in marriages. There will likely be money and assets coming out of the trust to one of the spouses. While such distributions are presumptively separate property of the beneficiary spouse, how the property is dealt with during the marriage needs to be addressed. It can't be disregarded when planning the terms of a prenup.

A spouse's interest in an irrevocable trust should be disclosed when entering into a prenup. The terms of the trust, especially the distribution terms for the future spouse, need to be thoughtfully analyzed. The possible distributions of principal at target dates need to be understood and the investments contained in the trust (the trust *corpus*) need to be disclosed, usually by means of a statement of assets. Past and expected distributions from the trust should be examined.

When dealing with a mediated prenup, I've found it extremely helpful to put the actual trust document on a Zoom screen to share with my clients and review the provisions of the trust that will be important to the marriage. I find that this educational process is beneficial to the trust beneficiary as well as to the marrying couple as a team. This is also a helpful exercise for the siblings of the beneficiary-spouse, who are educated by proxy by their sibling sharing this newfound understanding of the trust. People often don't understand what is actually in their trusts and what the rules of distribution might be. It should go without saying that this information is important to have if you are a trust beneficiary and the future spouse of one.

Another example of an important clause you may find in a trust is a "power of appointment." This is a provision that allows a beneficiary to choose who will receive the trust benefits that they have enjoyed when they die. Usually, the group of people that the beneficiary can choose from to receive this benefit is limited to the child's children or grandchildren, and if none, then the other descendants of the parents who set up the trust.

But sometimes, the class to which a beneficiary can appoint includes a spouse. Often the spouse's share will be required to be held in trust during the surviving spouse's lifetime. Often what is paid to the spouse is the income (but not the principal) of the trust. After the spouse's death, the remaining trust assets stay in trust to benefit the deceased beneficiary's children and further descendants. Knowing that there is a power of appointment option in the trust and what it can do is especially important for the couple. They now know that the trust beneficiary spouse can provide for the financial security of the other spouse after their death by means of exercising this power of appointment in their last will.

Some trust beneficiaries have accepted what their family advisors have told them — that the money in the trust is for their children and grandchildren, and that the money must travel down the bloodlines and be used sparingly for themselves or their own family. As a result, sometimes a trust beneficiary is leery about accepting money from the trust.

This may result in the nonbeneficiary spouse having to work hard their entire life to support the family, at the cost of not building up financial security for their own future. At the end of the marriage (or the death of the beneficiary spouse), the spouse who worked so diligently may be left with little. I've seen this happen. Knowing that the trust is being held separate and apart and is not benefitting both spouses in the marriage can be quite damaging.

There are problems that arise with the family irrevocable trusts. The trustees might not be generous in disbursing funds, or the beneficiary spouse does not advocate accepting money out of a sense of guilt. The result is that the new married couple may have little money with which to plan and invest for their own marriage. This reduces the agency of the marriage to control funds. As for the less-moneyed spouse, it is usually important (crucial really) to have adequate assets *outside* of the protected trust to secure that person if the marriage ends in divorce, and also at the time of the death of the beneficiary-spouse. A person can be left in a very unprotected situation.

Prenup terms can provide a backstop protection such that anything coming from third-party irrevocable trusts (including the trust corpus itself) cannot be claimed by an ex-spouse in a divorce. But what about planning for the income or any money generated by the trust during the marriage? Especially in a first marriage, accumulation of separate property during the marriage can have a negative effect. A plan to share funds coming out of a trust may be the best approach.

Many prenups provide that money that comes out of a trust is separate property, and is only shared within the marriage if the recipient spouse decides to share it. A prenup *can* require various plans for sharing of money coming out of trusts. It may stipulate that *all* money generated from the trust be shared in the marriage. Alternatively, it can provide that money below a certain target amount each year will be shared, and that the excess would stay the separate property of the recipient. That excess held as separate property (or some of it) may vest over time. This way both spouses can accumulate wealth.

The same considerations apply when there are not irrevocable family trusts set up before the marriage. Perhaps the wealthy parents of one of the future spouses intend to provide all or some of their child's legacy outright after their deaths (although this is a choice rarely made by parents who have great wealth). In defining the terms of the prenup, the couple should contemplate what to do about this eventual expectancy. They can adopt various sharing or vesting options in their prenup, like those involving treatment of trust distributions described above.

There are also family dynamics to consider when one of the spouses comes from a wealthy family. Many of these families have family wealth offices with teams of financial planners and lawyers who suggest (really, direct) how the children of these families should conduct their financial affairs. They may require a prenup be in place before the marriage and even require reviewing the terms and adding (and eliminating) terms before it is to be signed.

As a practical matter, the child of wealth (and their new future spouse) will need to accommodate the wishes and aims of these family professionals and keep peace. Fighting against them is like fighting against a riptide and will damage the goodwill between the family office (and perhaps the independent trustees) and the child of wealth. But having the discussions during the construction of the prenup is vitally important to creating a healthy framework for this family wealth.

Raising the issue of having a prenup as a requirement for marriage is itself usually upsetting for the couple. It's generally put forward by the wealthy parents or their advisors. It can be very upsetting to the parents of the less-moneyed future spouse. These parents find it insulting that the parents of their future daughter- or son-in-law wishes to hold financial benefits away from their child by means of a prenup. This has the potential of setting up negative dynamics before the wedding and often causes bad feelings and stress persisting well into the marriage.

Wealthy parents themselves also often agonize over whether to ask their child to get a prenup. I am routinely called upon by parents who are struggling with the issue of whether to ask their child to get a prenup, and if so, how best to do so. They clearly see the downsides of making such a request, and they are concerned with the effect on their child's (and the new spouse's) emotions.

Another factor to consider is the effect the prenup of a child of a wealthy family will have on their siblings. If that child is the first to marry in the family, that prenup might well serve as the template for all future sibling marriages. If they are not the first, it may be challenging for the new couple to depart from the prenup terms previously set by the other siblings.

It's important to know what would happen if there is no prenup. Although the law differs from state to state, in most states inherited property and property gifted by third parties (such as parents) during the marriage is considered separate property. This includes distributions from third party trusts. Third-party irrevocable trusts are a separate entity that are even not owned by the beneficiary spouse, and therefore, not even considered their "separate property." However, they need to be addressed in a prenup one way or another.

But even if the law "protects" inherited money and gifted money, it is possible to create conditions in a prenup that foster mutual parity during a marriage that exceeds the baseline provided by the law. Putting these terms (or some of them) into the prenup will benefit both parties, as it will create goodwill between the spouses and strengthen the financial bond of the marriage.

It's ironic that family wealth can pose problems in a marriage. Using a rational decision tree to navigate family wealth can give couples greater clarity and control over their choices. As with every other financial matter, when working on a prenup, inheritances from parents, and third-party trusts are issues that should be on the table. When they're discussed and when it results in authentic agreement between the couple, discontent about the financial terms of the marriage is greatly reduced, and a feeling of transparency and goodwill is fostered.

CHAPTER 14:

PRENUPS FOR BUSINESS OWNERS

O ne of the most frequent reasons people decide to have prenups is that they own, or have an interest in, a closely held ongoing business in which they actively participate, one that produces their livelihood. Sometimes this is a participation in a family business, owned by their parents or other relatives. In that case, the business might eventually become theirs. Sometimes it's a business that the future spouse has started themselves before the marriage. Some of these businesses may have other active partners or co-owners. People understandably do not want the claims of an ex-spouse to affect the control or operations of their business in the event of a divorce.

But keeping the results of one's business efforts and activity as separate property within a marriage can be a problem. It may distort what value each spouse contributes to the marriage. As the marriage proceeds, the unfairness can become more pronounced, detrimentally affecting a marriage. This is why state courts and case law value each party's contributions — whether they are at work, home, or a combination — as having equal value in a marriage.

The results of working in a business that you own (or partially own or will own in the future) has three components: salary (if the business is structured as an S corporation or C corporation), business profits, and the growth (hopefully) of the business's value over time. Much thought should be spent on how to address the economics of the ongoing business, especially should the marriage end in divorce.

Protection of a business is an important driving factor for having a prenup, and a very understandable one. In my law practice, I have seen the results of not protecting the control and ownership of a closely held family business because there was no prenup. In these cases, the nonbusiness-owning spouse can be awarded a part of the business, including a say in the control of the business. I've also read reported court cases dealing with the issue of how to fairly divide a significant business developed during a long-term marriage. These cases can involve multiple appeals and remands to lower courts, and they can go back to the higher courts in a process that can last upward of ten years and cost hundreds of thousands of dollars in legal fees.

So, if there is a family business involved, or if a future spouse is currently actively involved in a business that they control and have an ownership interest in (or will in the future), it's a good reason for having a prenup. The issue is how to compensate fairly the spouse who is not actively working in the business, without ceding control and ownership of the business from the active business-owner spouse.

The problem with many prenups is that this is often dealt with in an extreme manner that may leave a spouse out in the cold financially, even after a long marriage. One of the ways this occurs is to deem salary as marital property, but business profits as separate property. This way of looking at things can result in numerous negative consequences for the marriage, in addition to being unfair to the other spouse. Therefore, assets purchased or developed from earnings during the marriage are marital property.

Most state laws provide that earnings during marriage are marital. A critical issue to think about when one of the spouses is actively involved in a business that they own is how to classify what is "earned" income.

The business might be a sole proprietorship, or a C or S corporation. It may be a single- or multiple-person limited liability company or a partnership. (Note that limited liability companies can be treated as a sole proprietorship, a partnership, a C corporation, or an S corporation for tax purposes.) Some businesses, if there is one owner-operator, are considered "personal service businesses," in which the owner's earnings, even if called "profits," are tantamount to "salaries." But a problem arises when the business is one that distinguishes between an owner's salary and the profits of the business.

Let's say a person had a business that was operated as an S corporation and was earning $100,000 a year in salary. In addition to that, the business was generating $200,000 a year in profits. What happens if the prenup says that only "salary" is considered marital property in the marriage? I have seen many prenups with that term included. Having that term greatly affects the buildup of marital or community property during the marriage to the detriment of the other spouse.

Here's another problem: What if in the ten years since the marriage, the value of the business grows from $500,000 to $5 million and the prenup says that the value of the business itself is separate property? Is that fair to the other spouse who spent all their efforts (perhaps even including at the workplace) in furtherance of the marriage? How do these terms affect the quality of the marriage? It is obvious how these types of provisions can be harmful to marriages.

Sharing profits is healthy for a marriage. But sometimes a business owner needs to reinvest profits into the business for potential growth or to help it survive in hard times. Sharing the increase in value of the business during the marriage resolves the issue of "reinvesting in the business." Presumedly, the funds reinvested contributed to the business's growth or sustainability. That growth or survival benefits both spouses, assuming the value of the business itself is shared.

Sometimes the active business participant's salary is set at a low level, and the rest of the earnings are called "profits" to limit the social security tax that otherwise would be assessed. Or it might be set low because the owner of the business wishes to keep that profit income available for investing in separate assets. Or it was set to salary only because the owner of the business (the future spouse or the future spouse's parent) wants to protect the future profits from exposure to a possible divorce in the upcoming marriage.

But if it's done for any reason, it causes a problem. First, it creates a latent hoarding potential for the business spouse, because they now have separate property that may be growing and will be a priority for them. Especially in a first marriage, separate property tends to pull people apart and can weaken the marriage.

The other spouse will see their spouse's personal financial enrichment over time due to what they think are efforts that should be benefiting the marriage, not just the one spouse. This situation could make that spouse feel badly. Then, as is in many prenups, the increase in the value of the business during the marriage belongs exclusively to the business owner, which adds insult to injury.

The unfairness inherent in this situation makes that spouse think that perhaps they made a mistake in marrying the business spouse in the first place. Maybe it would have been better to marry someone that did not own a business, so that if a new business was started after the marriage, it would be a marital asset. The whole arrangement makes the marital relationship adversarial (think divorce) and upends the feeling of generosity and mutual contribution that sustains a marriage.

When there are other active or silent owners of the business, it provides additional complexity in how to structure the treatment of the financial aspects of the business when formulating a prenuptial agreement. Other structural issues include determining a fair appraised value of the business at the start of the marriage and at the time of divorce to assess any increase in value during the marriage. And when a spouse uses separate property to purchase, sustain, or grow the business, there are additional questions to address. Fortunately, determining the rules about how to treat profits generated by businesses in prenups is fairly straightforward.

But assessing business value is difficult. The business appraisal process is complex and expensive. Multiple appraisers can often come up with widely disparate values. The length of time it takes to get a formal appraisal can often be many months. Complications can arise if the business is controlled by a parent or other family member who may not want to reveal information about the business that would permit an appropriate appraisal. It is also likely that this person (often the future spouse's parent) is the person who asked their child to get the prenup in the first place.

In any case, a date of marriage value might be needed for purposes of the prenup. With adequate business records collected at the time of the marriage, the "start" value of the business at the time of marriage should be capable of being derived forensically. Any disputes can be resolved by binding arbitration, if the need arises, through an alternative dispute resolution (ADR) clause that I highly recommend be in any prenup.

One of the first steps in considering a prenup when business assets are involved is to seek a full disclosure regarding the business. If you are the future spouse who is an owner and works in the business, you should expect to disclose everything that is relevant to the ownership, value, and operation of the business. That will include tax returns of the business going back several years, as well as accounting reports such as profit-and-loss, revenue, and expense statements for at least the current year. Operating agreements, partnership agreements, and "buy-sell" agreements will need to be shared and evaluated as well. Sometimes information about a business as reported in the news will be helpful to understand the business's current trajectory.

Full and complete financial disclosure is necessary. It's good practice to over-disclose rather than under-disclose when negotiating a prenup with a business involved. (Actually, in any prenup, full and complete disclosure is a predicate to informed consent and enforceability.)

If a spouse will receive a share of the growth of a business during the marriage, it is important that the payment of the spouse's interest does not interfere with the operation or financial health of the business. In the event of a divorce, the business spouse will want to retain control of the business and not have the ex-spouse be their business partner. There are some exceptions, but this is generally the case. Therefore, the payment of the marital interest to the nonbusiness spouse will generally not be made as an ownership interest in the business, but through other marital assets. The payment terms need to be feasible for the business owner and reasonable and secure for the other spouse.

When providing payment to the nonbusiness spouse from assets other than the business, this payment can be made as a lump sum through a combination of assets, including retirement accounts. If there are not sufficient liquid assets at that time to make full payment, the prenup can address this eventuality by structuring the payment with a down payment and a contractual agreement to make periodic payments over time or pay the full balance at some future date. Details of this can be worked out at the time of a divorce, when all the facts are known. Any aspects not negotiated by the spouses can be resolved in binding arbitration at that time.

In addition to looking to the prenup for guidance when dealing with a spouse's share, if the marriage has ended through the death of the business spouse, the surviving spouse will also need to understand how this issue is addressed in the decedent spouse's estate plan. This is one reason I usually require an estate plan be executed at the same time as couples enter a prenup and a framework for the estate plan to be set forth in the prenup itself. (See Chapter 9.)

If there are other owners or partners involved in the business, there is likely to be a buy-sell or operating agreement that prevents third parties (such as surviving spouses and other family members of the deceased spouse) from gaining a controlling interest in the company. Usually, the beneficiary after death steps into the shoes of the decedent as to *distributions* from the business but will have no rights of control. Often the buy-sell agreements are funded by life insurance policies that can come into play if the spouse-owner dies. This allows the existing owners to buy out the surviving spouse's interest in the company.

It is clear that a prenup can be a valuable tool when a spouse is actively engaged in a business by providing predictability, clarity, and fairness should there be a time when that business is to be divided. A business interest can be protected (as well as the interest of other stakeholders) while still providing an equitable result to the nonbusiness spouse if all aspects are properly addressed within the prenup.

CHAPTER 15:

GRAY PRENUPS FOR SECOND MARRIAGES

You may remember the story of Cinderella. It's one that gets to the heart of what might happen in second marriages. Cinderella's mother dies, and her father marries a wicked stepmother, who favors her own daughters while treating Cinderella as a virtual slave in her father's house. She's not even permitted to go to the king's ball to have a chance to meet the prince and possibly be chosen as his bride.

Fast-forward several hundred years to today. A mother dies, and the father remarries. The new spouse also has children from her first marriage. The father doesn't think about the consequences of estate planning, and he wills his entire estate to his new spouse upon his death. The security, needs, and caring for the children of his first family seem to be forgotten and disregarded.

I've heard this story many times during my years of practicing law. Not being careful to plan for equity between the sets of adult children of a blended family can cause heartache for the children, as well as for the parents. Families can get torn apart over this. Parents can lose the respect of their children. Second marriages may weaken and break up. Enter the "gray prenup."

A new term for older couples getting divorced at mature ages is "gray divorce." Similarly, "gray prenup" is used to refer to prenups for people in their 50s, 60s, 70s, and beyond who are marrying again. "Gray prenups" (sometimes called "baby-boomer prenups") have their own issues, challenges, and opportunities.

Most older people getting married have children from previous marriages. Their financial loyalty tends to be divided between their children and their new spouse. As parents, they usually wish to leave a secure financial legacy for their children. But they also want to make sure that the financial situation between themselves and their new spouse is reasonable. And they want to make sure that there is peace between their children and their new spouse.

If their first spouse died, the person considering a prenup may consider any inheritance from part of the estate assets they accumulated during their marriage as really belonging to the deceased spouse. They might view that part of their estate as essentially "in trust" for the children of that prior marriage. They may feel they morally owe that legacy to the children of that marriage, and they will want to make sure that those children eventually receive it if it's not needed by the spouse who is entering this new marriage.

Parents naturally want to help their children establish themselves in life. Parents may wish to help their children by providing gifts, financial assistance, and assisting with the cost of their children's education, even if they enter into a second marriage. It's natural for people with children to want to give them a step-up in life.

When middle-aged people and seniors remarry, they sometimes marry people who are as financially secure as they are. On the other hand, in some cases their new partner is not financially secure. Because they love their new spouse, they will want to make sure their new spouse is secure and protected if they should die first. These situations lead to some very specific terms in a prenup. When the two people coming into the marriage are equally financially secure and don't need the financial protection of the other spouse, the terms of a gray prenup can be quite different.

When a second spouse needs financial protection after the death of a spouse, the couple needs to strike a balance between their financial loyalty to each other and their financial loyalty to the children from their previous marriages. Balancing these competing interests is a frequent challenge in later-in-life marriages and may be the primary reason to formulate a gray prenup.

Sound prenups should handle this balance in a sensible and coherent way. This can be done by formulating and memorializing the basic terms of a mutually conceived estate plan in a prenup.

There are many horror stories about seniors who remarry and disinherit their children in favor of their new spouse. Creating a reasonable balance of inheritance upon death goes a long way to creating goodwill between the children of one spouse and the new spouse. Creating intentional certainty of financial results in the marriage of senior newlyweds can preserve and enhance peace within the blended families. As a result, it can support, protect, and help sustain the new marriage as well.

In cases where a surviving spouse is independently financially secure, then the first-to-die may be able to leave their entire estate to the children of their prior marriage. But keep in mind that in some cases, the surviving spouse might still need protection.

Here's another issue to contemplate: What happens if a marriage ends in the death of one of the spouses where that spouse has received all the assets of the marriage and then remarries? If a spouse wishes their wealth to be passed down through their bloodlines, more planning is needed. Some spouses wish to give their surviving spouse free rein to marry again and to do what they wish to the assets they inherited from them. Their wish is for their surviving spouse to be happy, and if there are no prior children of the deceased, this can be a generous and legitimate goal. Some wish to give their estate (or part of it) through QTIP trusts or life estates, so that after the death of the second spouse, what remains of the property can go to their children.

Sometimes the financial needs of seniors themselves are the primary aim in a gray marriage because of lack of assets, income, and/or retirement assets of one or both spouses. It is important for spouses (even gray spouses) to take care of each other during their lives together. After all, one of the purposes of marriage is to support, sustain, and protect each other. If you care for your spouse, you want to do this. A prenup allows you to do this in an orderly and thoughtful way.

Another wrinkle in this situation may be how to manage lifetime gifts for grown children. Some children are quite self-sufficient and don't really need much (if any) financial help. Some children are not established or may have chronic livelihood issues or health problems affecting their means of support. These issues also can (and should) be addressed in a workable way by the new gray couple. It's a complicated issue but an important one to tackle.

People in this circumstance need to think about their current financial plan and also envision the future when one and then both spouses have died. For this type of planning, seeking counsel from an estate-planning attorney and putting a new estate plan in place is important. People need to be aware of the estate-planning options available to them, especially what happens if they die without a will.

Benefits can be accessed when seniors who are marrying enter into coordinated estate plans. The most important is that they can make use of each other's excess federal estate tax exemptions. This is done by using trusts (such as QTIP trusts and credit shelter trusts) and "porting" excess federal exemptions to a surviving spouse who may be able to utilize it to reduce estate taxes. It's not a *reason* to get married, but in many cases, the tax savings can be hundreds of thousands of dollars. These estate tax savings have a significant financial benefit overall that a less-moneyed spouse can bring to the marriage.

If in reasonably good health and not elderly, the spouses could obtain life insurance to secure an inheritance for their children or their new spouse. This can add to the choices available as to how to allocate their assets during their gray marriage and upon their death.

A question that arises for seniors who are remarrying focuses on how they use their income and assets to provide for their living expenses. Some couples like to share expenses by setting up shared accounts to which they will each contribute a determined amount or percentage each month. Some prefer to specify which sources of income will be used for sharing living expenses.

Often retirement income in a prenup for second marriages is characterized as "separate property." When people in gray second marriages use it to support their living expenses, they are converting their separate assets into marital assets. This sometimes is treated fluidly. Often one spouse may have significantly more retirement assets than the other. This may result in the one spouse generously paying a larger share of the couple's living expenses. Each couple will need to decide what they feel is an equitable way to draw down their assets to support themselves. They can also use income from other separate assets (and/ or the assets themselves) if, and as, needed for living expenses.

Some couples might want to analyze this sharing of expenses in detail and put some rules in the prenup about how they will allocate retirement income during their marriage. Perhaps they want to allocate proportions to be contributed by overall net worth, with the idea that this is a more equitable way to ultimately leave assets to the respective children of each of them. On the other hand, many couples choose to decide how they want to pay for shared expenses during their second marriage outside of a prenup, which allows for more flexible changes from time to time.

It's important to be informed about the benefits of leaving retirement assets to a surviving spouse (or part of them, anyway) if there will be an inheritance for that spouse. Under current law, nonspouse beneficiaries (for example, children) must take distributions of all the money in an inherited retirement account within ten years of the death of the parent who bequeathed the account to them. (There is an exception for disabled children.) All the money taken out is taxable as ordinary income when distributed to the beneficiary. So, leaving retirement assets to children is not a great way to leave a legacy to them. It's not tax-efficient. If they wanted to use it to buy a house, upward of 35 percent would be lost to their income tax bill when they withdraw the funds from the inherited retirement account.

When a *spouse* inherits a retirement account, the rules are very different. A surviving spouse can roll over the inherited retirement assets into their own IRAs and extend the payouts dramatically, depending upon their age. Under current law, a surviving spouse doesn't have to start withdrawing these benefits until age 73, and then they can withdraw them on a schedule as required minimum distributions (RMDs) during the rest of their life. If a spouse keeps the retirement benefits in an *inherited* IRA, they will need to begin taking RMDs the year after the death of their spouse, but they can delay beginning RMDs until the time at which the *deceased spouse* would have turned 73. Both of these treatments available to surviving spouses are much more favorable than what must happen if you leave IRAs to the nonspouse younger generations who are subject to the ten-year rule.

It's important to know for planning purposes that spouses have certain rights with respect to ERISA-qualified retirement accounts. These include 401(k) plans, 403(b) plans, and certain other retirement plans.

A surviving spouse must receive at least 50 percent of the benefits of these plans, unless a waiver is signed by that spouse *after* the marriage and before the death of the account-holder spouse. This waiver must be in the form required by the plan administrator and signed in front of a notary public. If you do this, verify that it was received by the plan administrator, so make sure you receive a confirmation.

If the waiver form is not signed, the surviving spouse will have the right to receive (and will receive) 50 percent of the plan's assets even if the mutual intent (and the terms of the prenup) was for the plan proceeds to be distributed elsewhere, such as to the children of the first marriage.

In some cases, the senior remarried couple may wish to accumulate some marital property that they will share during their marriage. This may be accumulated through income earned by working seniors. Or they may wish to change ownership of certain separate assets to joint ownership. The prenup will reflect what the spouses wish to do with this shared property after one of them dies or if there is a divorce. It might be that the couple decides that this shared money or assets will be bequeathed to the surviving spouse. Sometimes it's divided (often in half) at the last death between the heirs (usually the children) of the spouses.

Sometimes the development of marital property is needed for one of the gray spouses who has fewer assets than the other, to provide them with financial security, even if the marriage ends in divorce. This will need to be planned for, too, in an equitable and cogent way. But even if not strictly needed by either spouse, having marital property developed in a gray remarriage may have a positive emotional effect.

Another important consideration is what happens to the residence and living arrangements of the surviving spouse after the death of the first spouse, whether that residence is owned jointly or not. This can and should be addressed in a prenup.

A harsh provision that I've seen in some prenups (not the ones I've written), when the deceased spouse owned the house individually, is that the non-owning spouse must vacate the property within 30 or 60 days after the other spouse's death. But there are other, gentler ways to address this issue.

Decisions need to be made about whether the non-owner can stay in the home for a long or short period of time. There can be a generous term of months or years before the surviving spouse must leave the residence, after which the property can then go to the deceased spouse's heirs.

If the couple decides that there is enough money to satisfactorily distribute to the heirs of the deceased spouse, sometimes the prenup plan may provide the non-owning spouse a life estate in the residence (sometimes by means of a beneficial interest in a QTIP trust). A life estate is a title-holding mechanism in which the surviving spouse has the right to use and occupy the home (if owned by the deceased spouse) until their death. Then the property can go to the children of the deceased spouse. This life estate concept is imbedded in QTIP trusts and credit shelter trusts, which are standard estate-planning techniques whereby a surviving spouse can use assets during their lifetime, after which the remainder would go to the children of the deceased spouse. This technique of holding property for the use of the surviving spouse during their lifetime can apply to other assets also, such as securities accounts that are held in trust.

This means that person can stay in the home until they die. These options have estate tax ramifications that may be important in the estate-planning process. Their effect can be to lessen overall estate taxes, which might ultimately benefit the children of the deceased spouse as well as providing for the comfort and well-being of the surviving spouse.

If the home is jointly owned by the decedent spouse and the surviving spouse, decisions still need to be made. Some couples would like the surviving spouse to stay in the home, either for a term of years or for life, and afterward divide the proceeds of the house when sold. Any of these decisions should be spelled out in the prenup and confirmed by the execution of the appropriate estate-planning documents.

Other decisions involve what happens if a spouse leaves the home because they wish to relocate, or they need to relocate because they require more care. Does that spouse get continued support from the decedent's estate, or not? The couple may also determine in the prenup whether and to what extent operating costs of the residence (or a future residence occupied by the surviving spouse) will be paid for by the estate or through a trust of the decedent and which costs will be paid by the surviving spouse.

These are all topics that need to be discussed and understood during the premarital prenup process. Obviously, the conclusions will vary according to the financial circumstances of the spouses and their views as to how these choices should be resolved.

Nowadays, spouses in a gray marriage are sometimes faced with grown children that may need some financial support. Many parents also wish to make lifetime gifts for their children even if there is no actual need. Based on life expectancies, most legacies from parents come when the grown children are in their 50s. Often these children are financially established by that time, so it often makes sense to help children along when the children are younger and starting to establish their own households and careers. The new spouses in a second marriage can make decisions collectively about how to support and make gifts to their children during their marriage. They should give this careful thought and perhaps set guidelines regarding gift-giving in their prenup.

Sometimes there could be an asset pool established for gifts and assistance to children available to distribute annually. It would be in an amount that the spouses agree upon, and the amounts could be changed from time to time by mutual decision. Or there could be two separate pools of shared income for gifts for each of the spouses to make for their own children. If there is one child of one of the spouses that requires extra assistance, spouses should be aligned in the amount of help they want to provide that child. Gifts that are greater than the pool can be made from separate assets of that spouse to their children.

In some gray prenups, spousal support for the less-moneyed spouse can be an important consideration for that spouse, if the marriage ends in divorce. This should be thought through, and a fair solution should be reflected in the terms of the prenup. How long the support would last, the amount, and its sources could be prescribed in a gray prenup. Sometimes this might be necessary even after the age when most pay-ors of alimony would not have the obligation (e.g., after retirement).

"Alimony" tends to be a hot word. Most spouses who have had to pay it feel burned. But thinking about the ultimate well-being of the spouse you are marrying at the prenup stage, even if it is a "gray" marriage, is a good thing and may increase the probability that the marriage will last.

One of the realistic worries people have going into a gray marriage is the chance that one of them will become mentally or physically dis-abled to the extent they will no longer be able to be taken care of in their own home or by their spouse. Anyone marrying later in life runs the risk of ending up in a nursing home — sometimes for an extended stay.

Although this won't happen to everyone, when it does, it is a significant financial drain. Skilled nursing facilities are expensive.

Medicare pays only up to twenty days per illness fully, and up to another 80 days with a co-payment. If you don't have coverage through a Medigap insurance policy or a long-term care insurance policy, it's an expensive proposition. Home care, if needed, is also expensive. It might be needed 24/7, even if the other spouse is still living in the home.

A long stay in a nursing home (or extended need for significant home care) can deplete the financial assets of any couple, including a couple in a gray marriage. It can wipe out a lifetime of savings. It is difficult to get long-term nursing insurance after a certain age; policy premiums are rising astronomically, and many companies are no longer offering this type of insurance.

People entering gray marriages often wonder who is responsible for nursing home costs if one of them needs to go into a skilled nursing facility for a protracted time — perhaps up until their death. Current rules stipulate that the spouse not in the nursing home (called the "community spouse") is required to pay the other spouse's nursing home costs, once the assets of the spouse in the nursing home are depleted to the sum of $2,000.

Under current law, when one spouse enters a nursing home, the community spouse is only permitted to retain 50 percent of the couple's assets, up to a maximum of $154,140, and the right to stay in the marital home. And a prenup cannot be used for the community spouse to avoid financial responsibility for nursing home costs. For Medicaid purposes, the gray spouses are viewed as one entity, therefore jointly responsible. State and federal laws supersede the private contract provisions you make in a prenup regarding who should pay for these expenses.

There are some estate-planning possibilities that might be available to use to protect a spouse's assets. (For this, an experienced "elder law" attorney should be consulted.) Sometimes the only possibility is a "Medicaid divorce." Elders who are in a second or later marriage need to look at their assets and see if each (or if one of them) can comfortably pay for extended nursing care. There are outliers who spend ten or twenty years in a skilled nursing facility; however, statistically it is very rare that a person spends more than three years in one.

Unmarried people living together are not responsible for paying the nursing home costs of their partner. So, if you are thinking of getting married at an advanced age, it is important to evaluate the financial risk of marrying. Most people assume the risk and marry anyway, because marriage (as opposed to living together) is important to them emotionally as well as in many other ways.

If you decide not to marry, you may decide to arrange the financial relationship between you and your partner in an agreement, often called a "Living Together" agreement or a "Cohabitation and Property" agreement. Although these are beyond the scope of this book, you should be aware that prenuptial agreements are made "in contemplation of marriage." Depending on where you live, your "Living Together" agreement is likely to be deemed terminated and have no force and effect once you legally marry. Consult with an attorney if you find yourself in that situation.

A tender topic for people entering second marriages is what and how many details to share with your children. Should you tell them you will have a prenup and leave it at that? Or if not, how much detail should you provide?

It is usually appropriate and helpful to let grown children know that their parent is considering a prenup or has entered into one with the new spouse in a gray marriage. Details of exactly what is in the prenup can be provided or not, depending on the family dynamics and situation.

Certainly, the subject of having a prenup can be articulated in general terms. A parent might frame the discussion by saying, "We have set the terms of our prenup so that we will support each other during our lifetimes, and after we die, all of you (all the children) will share in what's left of our estate." Or "When I die, you will receive part of your inheritance, even if Jane is still living. After Jane dies, you will receive the rest of your inheritance." Or "I have put property in trust for Jane to support her after I die, but I expect there to be money left over for you three children after Jane dies."

A good strategy (if there is enough money to provide adequate security for the gray spouse) is to at least give some of your children's legacy to them at the time of your death, even if "Jane" is still alive. Letting the children know that you have considered them in your planning will be helpful for creating peace within the newly extended family.

Prenups are a strategic way to do thoughtful financial planning when embarking on a second marriage. It's not a "one-size-fits-all" proposition, and many gray marriages may not need one. But when needed and used thoughtfully, they can reduce conflict between the spouses and between the children of the spouses and their parents and provide a sound financial roadmap for the future.

CHAPTER 16:

ALIMONY: EVERYONE HATES IT

A limony is a highly charged word. Even when attorneys and mediators try to tamp down emotions by calling it "spousal support," it raises strong negative reactions on both sides of the alimony divide. It is indeed a hot-button issue.

Men (usually the payors) are generally outraged that after a marriage is over, they still must pay support to their former wives. This can occur even if the marriage ends because of a wife's unfaithfulness. A man might well complain, "Why should I pay alimony when I no longer have the services of my wife?" It just doesn't make sense to him.

Women, too, dislike the idea of alimony, because it represents an unwanted tie to a husband that they would prefer is out of their lives. It also smacks of an uncomfortable dependency. Hence, "alimony" has become an insulting word for women, too. Young women often believe alimony is a vestige of the past. They are often eager to sign prenups that include a waiver of alimony to prove their *bona fides* as independent, modern women.

People entering into prenups agonize over the issue of alimony, perhaps more than any other issue. Talking about it when formulating a prenup brings up strong feelings for both future spouses. But sometimes, even these days, spousal support may be a financial necessity after a marriage ends. This issue must be thought about and addressed when embarking on a prenup.

Because alimony *is* sometimes needed, there are laws in every state that provide for alimony to support an ex-spouse under certain factual situations. There are variations in the law as to when alimony is triggered and how to calculate its amount and duration. But no jurisdiction to date has barred a soon-to-be-divorced spouse from making a claim for alimony, which may be provided under appropriate circumstances.

There's some historical context to consider here. In the past (actually, not so long ago), a woman basically gave up her legal existence when she married. She had no right to own property on her own. Anything she earned or inherited during the marriage legally belonged to her husband. He had the right to control any income generated from her real estate or any other property during his lifetime. She could not sign a contract on her own nor incur debt without her husband's permission. She could not sue or be sued in court. She also could not directly share in the accumulation of assets during marriage. Even upon her husband's death, her rights to marital property were limited. The term for that was "coverture." The married woman's legal existence merged with and became part of the legal existence of the husband upon marriage. It became "covered" by the husband's existence.

In those times, women's means to survive economically outside of marriage were limited. Complicating this was that state laws made divorce next to impossible. Marriage was universally viewed as a religious sacrament and was indissoluble except under extreme circumstances. Sometimes it took a legislative act to get a divorce.

Counterbalancing this condition of women's extreme dependence on the financial decisions and control by men in their lives, husbands had the legal duty to support their wives during marriage and upon separation or divorce. It was understood as part of the marital contract that the wife had a duty to provide domestic services to the husband and childcare for her family.

As a result of this dependency, if a marriage ended, alimony was a necessity. It would continue until the woman remarried and was under the care and protection of another husband. This concept of alimony, ending at the remarriage of an ex-wife, has survived to this day, either by state statute or by legal custom. In modern times, some divorce agreements do not have this termination trigger, due to the "partnership" analysis of marriage. (See discussion below.)

This situation of dependency lingered into the 1970s. Even then, married women were usually unable to obtain credit or a mortgage without the consent of their husband. With the enactment of the Equal Credit Opportunity Act of 1974, a woman could apply for credit on her own. Before then (and slowly lessening thereafter), women's opportunities in the workforce were limited, and there were substantial barriers to advancing in their fields.

Now women make up a significant part of the workforce and have more opportunities to rise in employment status than ever before. Still, because of family demands and often taking time off from full-time work to raise a family, women's lifetime and hourly earnings are statistically depressed. (Usually, but not always, it's the woman who devotes herself primarily to home management.) When there is a family, there's usually a primary breadwinner, and that's usually the husband.

A modern perspective is that the right to alimony is a contractual right to a share of the other spouse's income derived from the economic partnership of marriage. In this partnership analysis, alimony can be seen as compensation for loss of earning capacity due to having and raising children and performing the greater part of the household duties and making and managing a home life.

Another legal doctrine underlying this situation is termed *promissory estoppel*. It occurs when someone makes a promise and another person, who reasonably relies on the promise, changes their position and suffers a financial loss as a result. The person who made the prom-ise is legally "estopped" by a failure to stand by it. That's the reason it's called *promissory estoppel.*

To receive a promissory estoppel award for damages (unless vol-untarily given by the person who made the promise), there must be a lawsuit. In the case of divorce and compensation for leaving the job market to have a family and resulting depressed earnings, the lawsuit is the divorce action itself. In it, the court evaluates the loss when alimony (and sometimes property division) is determined.

But alimony does sting. Sometimes, a paying spouse is fully employed and working hard, and the other spouse might not be work-ing up to his or her economic capacity, or not working at all. Perhaps the children are grown and out of the home. In this case, the spouse might be middle-aged (or older) and have no realistic job prospects or experience.

A former spouse in their 50s or 60s *can* go back to work as an entry-level employee in a service- or retail-related job. But is that evenhanded or fair after a long marriage, especially if the other spouse has a well-paid professional or business position, having achieved an excellent career trajectory during the marriage with the wife as their helpmate?

The issue of unfairness is often deeply felt by a potential payor spouse when embarking on a second marriage. He may have felt that he was unfairly burdened by the alimony payment after his prior mar-riage. Addressing this is an especially tender issue in prenups and can be one of the motivating factors to get one.

But the potential recipient spouse also hates alimony. There's that awful feeling of dependency, a perceived lack of respect, and a loss of control. There are also diminished possibilities to move forward into another stable relationship, since in most divorces, alimony ends if the recipient remarries. That means a former spouse might be financially "stuck," feeling the need to remain unmarried. On both sides of the alimony divide, most divorced people feel anger and angst about its presence in their lives.

The right to spousal support can be waived in a prenup. The parties might both be professionals or businesspeople with substantial incomes and/or assets. They may be highly employable. In these cases, there may be little risk to either party to agree to an alimony waiver. Or they might be in a later-in-life marriage, in which each of the parties is financially secure.

But in most cases, is waiving alimony a thoughtful and wise thing to do?

Because of the difficulty of foreseeing the future, courts have tended to be wary of absolute waivers of alimony in prenups, especially in prenups of younger people in first marriages. When you marry at 30, you simply don't know what your situation will be at 55 or 60 or 70.

What if events change and one party becomes ill and can no longer work? What if there is a major business downturn or bankruptcy? What if something unanticipated happens? Knowing that there is an alimony waiver in the prenup can increase the instability of the marriage. The idea that support is impossible often triggers intensely negative emotions in the disadvantaged spouse at the outset, thereby making divorce more likely as time goes on. They may feel trapped.

Shouldn't couples have a reasonable right to divorce if appropriate for them? Even with couples in a seemingly financially secure position, a prenup could include a provision to reevaluate the waiver if there is a substantial change of circumstances. And in some cases, an alimony waiver in a prenup may be disallowed by a court. (See Chapter 17 for more detail about enforceability of alimony waivers.)

At the time of a marriage, parties presumably care very much about each other and feel responsible for each other's well-being. Part of this care should be to think about and plan for an alimony provision in the prenup that is workable and reasonable. There are a number of possibilities to consider aside from a complete waiver. These include a partial waiver, with various trigger points and multiple methods of calculation that can be written into the prenup.

The possibilities also include no waiver at all. This means the prenup would leave the issue of alimony open to resolution under state law provisions in the state where the divorce occurs. In many ways, this is the optimal way to handle the issue in first marriage prenups. But a few states are very restrictive in what alimony payments would consist of and the duration of such payments.

Alimony law is supposed to be fair and reasonable based on the factual situation at the time of divorce. Divorce law generally considers many factors in determining amount and duration. Foremost among them, length of marriage, earning capacity of each party, needs of the supported party, and the ability of the supporting party to pay spousal support.

There are many ways to create rules or guardrails in the alimony terms of prenups to provide some guidelines. Some prenup alimony provisions provide that separate property and income from separate property will *not* be considered when determining the amount of alimony awarded. Some include (or don't include) income from marital assets that have been divided in determining the alimony amount. In some prenups, only a party's earned income through employment will count in the determination.

But what if the potential payor has no earned income, perhaps because they are retired or have family wealth and don't need to work? Is it really fair for that person's separate assets, which generate ample income (say it's in the millions), to be inaccessible to provide a safety net for the other spouse? That's what could happen if there is waiver of alimony in that prenup.

Some prenups ensure that enough assets are conveyed to a dependent spouse (including perhaps a dwelling) to keep that spouse in an appropriately comfortable situation if the marriage ends in divorce. This settlement option could begin after a certain number of years of marriage, or it could phase in gradually. Another possibility is to draw a fence around the alimony issue by having alimony paid for a shorter duration and/or for a lesser amount than the alimony laws would otherwise establish under state law.

Sometimes a "standard of living" could be required when determining the amount of alimony. It could be articulated as the standard of living prior to the marriage, the standard of living enjoyed at the end of the marriage, or a standard somewhere in between. This could be very specific, including comparative residential neighborhood or price ranges of a house or condo that would be financially feasible for an ex-spouse to reside in (or have outright ownership of). This can be set forth under the divorce terms of the prenup. The price range could be adjusted over time by applying the change in an appropriate housing price index.

Even in many gray prenups, spousal support can be important for a spouse if the marriage ends in divorce. In some gray marriages, as in other marriages, one of the spouses may be financially dependent on the other. When you marry, you need to think about the well-being of your spouse, even if the marriage ends in divorce. That type of caring at the prenup stage is a good thing and may increase the mutual feelings of generosity that sustain a marriage from the beginning. I've seen gray prenups where both spouses have careers and/or assets in which there would be a lump sum payment in lieu of alimony to rehome a spouse after a divorce. It can be a caring and generous thing to do.

There exists an interplay in the law between the calculations of spousal support and child support. However, a prenup cannot determine the amount or duration of child support or deal with child custody issues. The court has the final say in all child-related issues, which are determined based on the "best interests of the child." Child support, child custody, and visitation are issues of public policy over which the court retains jurisdiction.

• • •

There are many ways to think about how to structure alimony in your prenup. It's best to create a fair and reasonable outcome even if not required by law, as in those states in which alimony waivers are only invalidated if "unconscionable." (See Chapter 17.) Having a fair and sound alimony plan not only supports the enforceability of the prenup, but it also demonstrates caring and creates goodwill between the spouses at the time of marriage and beyond.

ARE ALL PRENUPS ENFORCEABLE?

No, not all of them. But probably 99.9 percent of them *are*. It's difficult to invalidate a prenuptial agreement. They are overturned only in the most fact-egregious cases. If you are going to sign a prenup, you should assume it will last for your entire marriage and will go into effect without change at death or divorce, even if you are the less-advantaged future spouse and you did not sign it precisely "voluntarily."

Only under the most appalling circumstances might a prenup be invalidated. The scenario would be something like this:

He tells her, "We need to go to my lawyer's office to sign paperwork for our wedding tomorrow." She's from another country, and her English is not very good. The paperwork is a prenup — a highly restrictive one — and she signs it. The prenup may be technically unenforceable, but when the marriage breaks up, she probably won't have enough money to fund the litigation.

Coercion, duress, and overreaching are grounds for finding a contract unenforceable. Since a prenup is a contract, they apply.

The person claiming unenforceability has the burden of proof, which means they must convince a court of their claim. Generally, the standard of proof to overturn a prenup on these grounds is high — it needs to be proven by clear and convincing evidence. That means the evidence must make the claim substantially and exceedingly likely to be true. In normal contract law, the burden of proof is generally a much weaker standard — by the preponderance of evidence. A preponderance means that only a 51 percent chance that the claim is true is required.

What is coercion? It occurs if someone tries to persuade another to do something using force or threats. The force or threats do not have to be physical. They can be psychological, including harassment and intimidation. In a prenup, the threat is that if the future spouse does not sign the prenup, there will be no marriage. For coercion to exist, the party submitting to signing the contract must act in a way so contrary to their own interests that the person is not deemed able to act with their own free will. You can imagine how difficult that would be to prove in the context of someone signing a prenup, albeit unhappily, which is often the case.

Duress is similar to coercion. It involves actual or threatened peril so severe that it overcomes the mind of a person. It leads to someone making choices against their free will or better judgment, limiting the person's ability to make a free choice. Again, it is extremely difficult to prove in the context of a prenup.

Overreaching is similar to coercion and duress. It is defined as taking unfair advantage of another's vulnerability. It happens when there is an inequality of bargaining power or other circumstances in which there is an absence of meaningful choice on the part of one of the parties. That sounds similar to the situation at the inception of many prenups. If one of the parties to the contract is the grossly disproportionate beneficiary of the transaction, it raises questions of overreaching. But as you will see below, most of the legal rules on prenup enforceability allow disproportionate terms in prenups as acceptable, making overturning a prenup on this legal ground very unlikely.

In many cases, the amount of time between the presentation of the agreement and the wedding date is significant because it may bear on whether there has been a meaningful opportunity to obtain the advice of counsel before signing. Short time frames can also suggest the presence of coercion. This is true especially if the prenup provides disproportionately less than a party would have received in a divorce without a prenup.

But, in general, prenups can be signed just before a wedding. This is usually when prenups are signed by prepared, informed parties who have been represented by attorneys; where the prenup is not excessively one-sided; and when there had been significant negotiations occurring before the signing. When one person is not represented by counsel and the prenup is disadvantageous to that person, the validity of the agreement may be in question.

Contracts, including prenups, can be invalidated if there is a fraud that influences a party's decision to sign it. Lack of financial disclosure can rise to the level of fraud if it's intended to mislead the other party. Misrepresentation of assets and liabilities in negotiating a prenup can be deemed fraudulent. There also may be fraudulent concealment, which is when someone hides an important fact from another person on purpose with the intention of misleading them. Fraud and fraudulent concealment are difficult to prove because there must be clear and convincing evidence — a very high standard.

In the commercial contract context, parties have no special duty to each other. They can treat each other "at arm's length," and the doctrine of *caveat emptor* ("buyer beware") applies (although fraud and fraudulent concealment are actionable). But there are important differences between prenups and commercial contacts. States view prenups as contracts that have public policy requirements because the parties are going to be *married*. Marriage is viewed as a special relationship that the state wishes to protect and sustain that goes far beyond a conventional business contract.

Once a couple is married, each of them has the legal duty to act in each other's best interests. This includes being responsible for their spouse's best *financial* or economic interests. That makes sense, because you're married. This obligation is called a "fiduciary duty." (It is sometimes legally termed a "confidential" relationship.)

When you have a fiduciary duty, you are subject to a high standard of care toward the other person. For example, attorneys have a fiduciary duty to their clients. They must act in their clients' best interest, not their own. Similarly, trustees have a fiduciary duty to act in the trust's beneficiaries' best interests. People have reason to trust the financial actions of a person who is acting as their fiduciary. It's a much higher standard of duty than the *caveat emptor* owed to people negotiating standard business contracts.

One would think that an engaged couple (sometimes having already been in a committed long-term relationship) would be presumed to have a fiduciary duty to each other at the time of negotiating their prenup, but state laws do not necessarily support this. And when negotiating a prenup that has an unfavorable term for your future spouse — even though you might not be acting in their best interest — by and large the prenup will be enforceable. The logical incongruity is keenly felt by both of the contracting future spouses.

There's another difference between prenups and business contracts. In every business contract there must be an exchange of consideration. In other words, one person gives something of value, and the other pays or gives something in exchange for it. The idea is that the exchange must be an equal trade.

But in prenup law, both in the uniform acts (which are incorporated into many state's laws) and in the academic treatises (which influence state laws and court cases), consideration is not required for a prenup to be enforceable. That's a glaring exception to standard contract law. It seems odd to have no consideration for the most important financial (and personal) contract most people ever make in their lives. The reasoning behind this is that the marriage *itself* is deemed the consideration for the negative terms the other spouse may be agreeing to in a prenup.

But is that realistic? If both parties are providing consideration by marrying each other, doesn't that shortchange the spouse who also relinquishes important financial rights? It sounds to me as if someone is being doubly compensated for the marriage and the other person is paying twice.

How can you place a monetary value on the contributions spouses give to each other in their marriages? And how can you know who is going to provide nonmonetary value or services to the other in the short term or in the future? How can you know that the value of the more-moneyed spouse's income and assets is worth more than the contributions (monetary and personal) that the other spouse will be making? Who knows who's going to help whom when the spouses are 75 or 80 years old? In many prenups, as one court bluntly put it, it could be that the future spouse was "selling herself" for an agreement resulting in a grossly disproportionate gain to the other party.

Remember that the word "consideration" in its normal usage means showing concern for the feelings of others. (See Chapter 10 for more on this.) When people are getting married, they generally want to be kind to each other. Bargaining about money right before the wedding is usually very distressing.

More than half of our states have adopted the Uniform Premarital Agreement Act of 1983, or variations of it. This act has a pro-prenup enforceability standard that benefits the more-moneyed party. The burden of proof is placed upon the person challenging the validity of the prenup, no matter what the circumstances are. To overturn the prenup, the prenup must be "unconscionable" at the time of the signing. (The

Act is silent as to a prenup's enforceability if the result is unconsciona-ble at the time it goes into effect at divorce.) Many other states that have not adopted the Act also employ the concept of unconscionability at the signing as a requirement to invalidate a prenup.

What is that unconscionability standard? Well, it's an extremely difficult standard to meet. In most state laws, the unconscionability must exist at the time of the *signing*, not at the time of enforcement. State case law defines what "unconscionability" means. The word, of course, is derived from something that is antithetical to someone's (or a court's) conscience. It is *un*-conscionable. Some definitions tie it to a lack of a sense of morality of what is right and wrong. It's the opposite of "conscience," which entails a strong sense of right and wrong and an urge to do the right thing.

Here's what the courts say:

- The inequality must be so strong and manifest as to shock the conscience.
- The terms must be so extremely unjust, or overwhelmingly one-sided in favor of the party who has the superior bargain-ing power, that they are contrary to good conscience.
- An unconscionable contract is held to be unenforceable because no reasonable or informed person would otherwise agree to it.
- An agreement is unconscionable when the "inequality is so strong, gross, and manifest that it must be impossible to state it to one with common sense without producing an excla-mation at the inequality of it." [This is one of my favorites.]
- An unconscionable agreement shocks the conscience of the court.

- An unconscionable agreement requires a greater showing of inappropriateness than a contract that is merely unfair and unreasonable.
- And from an eighteenth-century English case, the classic lawyer's definition: An agreement that "no man [sic] in his senses and not under delusion would make on the one hand and as no honest and fair man would accept on the other." *Earl of Chesterfield v. Janssen*, 28 Eng. Rep. 82, 100 (1750).

Unconscionability does not exist just because you made a bad deal or made a mistake in judgment. It doesn't exist merely because in retrospect you think that some of the provisions were improvident or one-sided. A prenup can be very "unfair," but that doesn't make it unconscionable. Prenups can and do result in a marital property settlement that a judge would not think right under a decree of divorce, but that doesn't make them unconscionable. The same is true about inheritance provisions in a prenup — they are often much more parsimonious than the laws would otherwise allow.

In light of this exacting standard, there are very few cases in which a contesting spouse has prevailed in a lawsuit contesting the terms of a prenup on the basis of unconscionability.

And it's even worse than merely having to prove unconscionability at the time of signing. In many states that have adopted the unconscionability standard, the spouse who wants to have the prenup invalidated must also prove that the financial disclosure had not been reasonable, that they did not voluntarily waive it beyond what was provided, and that they did not have, or reasonably could not have had, adequate knowledge of the property or financial obligations of the other party. Added to this, of course, would be the difficulty for the less-moneyed spouse to pay the cost required to mount any litigation (perhaps through appeals courts) necessary to find the prenup unenforceable.

A minority of states require that the terms of a prenuptial agreement be "fair and reasonable" at the time of signing rather than "not unconscionable." An even fewer number of these same states require that the "fair and reasonable" standard also be met at the time of enforcement.

Some but not all states protect spouses where circumstances have changed so far beyond the contemplation of the parties when they signed the prenup that the result may not be what the parties intended at the time it was executed. But even these states may provide insufficient remedies, sometimes just limited to making sure the former spouse does not become a public charge, that is, that they do not need to receive welfare or other government benefits for their support.

A prenuptial agreement generally requires full disclosure of assets, income, and liabilities. Full disclosure is important to the enforceability of prenups. Standards of disclosure vary from state to state. In many states, a party to a prenuptial agreement can waive their right to disclosure. In some states, even if the disclosure at the outset was not "fair and reasonable," the prenup would have had to have been "unconscionable" at the time of the signing to invalidate it.

When a prenup is signed, the financial disclosure portion should appear as an exhibit that becomes part of the prenuptial agreement. It should include an accurate list of assets, liabilities, income, and expectancies of future inheritances, as well as any anticipated changes in any of these areas and any contingent liabilities or reasonable expectations of additional assets or income. An example of the latter would be the disclosure of ongoing negotiations to sell a business that would result in proceeds for the future spouse above the business value stated in the prenup.

If there are third-party irrevocable trusts benefiting a future spouse, they need to be fully described in the financial disclosure. It's good policy to also give an estimate of any inheritance that the spouses may expect to receive from their parents in the future. This is usually expressed as a monetary range.

For purpose of the negotiations, it's important for the client and his or her attorney to look at actual underlying financial documents. These will include personal income tax returns, business income tax returns, financial account statements, business and asset valuations, financial statements, trust instruments, asset lists, and the like. Due diligence is important when negotiating prenups, and you will need the assistance of counsel. This requires sophisticated financial and tax expertise on the part of the attorney. It also requires an ability to explain complex financial issues to a client who may not be well versed in this area, especially if there are financial complexities involved.

The more complete and accurate the disclosure, the better. It serves to clarify the agreement being made and provides protection to both parties. The disclosure also helps to identify separate property and marital property as the marriage proceeds.

Alimony is one of the most difficult issues for people to contemplate when negotiating a prenuptial agreement. (See Chapter 16 for a full discussion and planning possibilities.) The right of alimony can be waived in a prenup. But should it be? There are questions of enforceability that apply to prenups with alimony waivers.

Because of the difficulty of foreseeing the future, courts have tended to be wary of absolute waivers of alimony in prenups, especially in prenups of younger people in first marriages. You don't know when you marry at a relatively young age what the future will hold. Your marriage may last 50 years, and many changes could happen during that time.

On the face of it, it seems that alimony would be an excellent candidate as an issue to be settled in a prenuptial agreement. It's something that many people seeking prenups are most interested in having in their prenup, especially if they feel burned by a prior divorce. However, some state courts and judges will not necessarily enforce alimony waivers, based on public policy concerns involving the financial well-being of former spouses.

These concerns are like the policy concerns regarding children — child support and child custody issues cannot be predetermined by a prenup. States do not readily relinquish their oversight role in protecting dependent spouses or children.

Having said that, alimony waivers in prenups are allowed in many states, and they are allowed with certain controls in others. In other states, they may be permitted depending on the relevant facts at the time of the execution of the prenup and/or at the time of divorce. In other words, in those states an alimony waiver might not be void *per se* but voidable under certain circumstances. The voidability often hinges on whether the waiver in that circumstance would be in violation of "public policy."

In some states, alimony waivers require that the person waiving the alimony have legal counsel before agreeing to the waiver. In others, they may be permitted to waive if they didn't have counsel, but the validity of the waiver would depend on the factual issues at the time of the execution of the prenup or the situation at the time of divorce.

In some states, the rule is that an alimony waiver may not be enforced if the prenup leaves the dependent ex-spouse without sufficient property and/or appropriate income or employment to support him or herself. This does not mean support in the style that the spouse was accustomed to during the marriage. That's the standard that applies in divorces where there is no prenup. But when there is a prenup, the level of the standard of living can be set much lower and still be enforceable. Virtually all states will deem an alimony waiver unenforceable if it leaves the dependent ex-spouse relying on public assistance for support.

• • •

A prenup that is not extreme or economically harsh at the time it is signed, and as it plays out during the marriage, will be more acceptable to the less-moneyed spouse. As a result (aside from a possibly more felicitous marriage), a spouse will be less likely to wish to contest the prenup. Also, both parties will find security in feeling that the prenup is a sound and workable contract that is beneficial to both of them and to their marriage as time goes on.

CHAPTER 18:

THE POSTNUPTIAL AGREEMENT: HANDLE WITH CARE

P ostnuptial agreements are essentially prenuptial agreements that are signed *after* the marriage. Postnuptial agreements are a relatively new area of law. They have been around for about 25 years. Most people have heard about prenups. Postnups are unfamiliar to most, and they are infrequently used. Prenuptial agreements are rare. Postnuptial agreements are even rarer. Almost all states now allow them. Postnups have the potential of being more perilous and subject to abuse than prenups, but they can still serve a useful function.

People are already married when they consider a postnup. When spouses are married, they have entered into a fiduciary relationship with each other. This entails the obligation to act in each other's best interests, including each other's best financial interests. (See Chapter 17.) Postnups are almost always drawn up to address finances. The danger is that they can result in impaired financial loyalty to a spouse in a process that can be less than "at arm's length."

As a result of the possible abuses and risks inherent in postnups, higher standards of protection apply than might apply to prenuptial agreements in many states. In these states, courts will scrutinize a postnuptial agreement to make sure it is fair and equitable or reasonable at the time of execution. Many courts also carefully scrutinize the results of a postnup at the time they go into effect at a divorce.

For this, a judge might consider the magnitude of disparity between the outcome under the postnup and what would happen under divorce laws *without* a postnup. This analysis might be especially acute in the case of long-term marriages. Also, the fact that an attorney had represented the spouse who is giving up rights will be very important in a judicial review. This is different from the laws of prenuptial agreements, which, overall, are unrestrictive, *laissez faire*, and end up being much less protective of spouses.

There are, however, other states where the laws of postnups are more hands off, providing greater latitude as to what can (and cannot) be in a financial contract for an ongoing marriage. In these states, the standard for a postnup to be invalidated are only that the agreement is not "unconscionable." (See Chapter 17 for a description of this very high standard.)

Another concern that arises about postnuptial agreements is that they have the potential to be coercive, because they usually arise when a marriage is failing and close to divorce. That can change the nature of the mutual bargaining that can occur in the context of negotiating the agreement. One spouse may give up a lot (maybe too much) by signing a postnup in their attempt to keep the marriage and family intact.

For these reasons, some states (by their laws and court decisions) are very concerned when enforcing postnups. In these states, courts may find them unenforceable more frequently than is the case with prenups. Postnuptial agreements in these jurisdictions are required to be more "generous" than prenups, more like a divorce settlement agreement than a prenuptial agreement, or somewhere between the two. A judge might scrutinize its terms very carefully to ensure that no coercion played a part in the postnup's formulation and signing.

At this time, postnuptial agreements (with the proper facts) can be found enforceable in virtually all states. Courts understand that some of these can help marriages survive through difficult times. They can serve a useful function in permitting married parties to address and arrange their financial affairs as they best see fit when circumstances change in the course of a marriage.

Usually, a discussion about having a postnup is triggered by some specific occurrence that disturbs the marriage and shakes its equilibrium. If it's not infidelity (see discussion below), it usually has something to do with money and security. When that comes up, it's often in a long-term marriage of 20 years or more.

Here are some examples of the situations that may be addressed by postnups:

Elliot, a spouse, was the major breadwinner in the family. Like many "breadwinner" spouses, he lost his job in the 2008 recession. Many of these (mostly) men were unable to be reemployed with earnings remotely commensurate with their pre-2008 earnings. They spiraled down in the job market, some permanently. Many had to take jobs at lesser salaries and not in the fields in which they had previously worked.

So, Elliot decides to go into business for himself rather than being permanently relegated to a job far below his experience and ability.

His spouse, Melissa, is risk averse. She doesn't want to put the money they have saved for retirement during their 25-year marriage into a new business venture. (New businesses are notorious money losers with a high failure rate.) She wants Elliot to just go out and get a salaried job, even if it pays less. She'll work more hours in her part-time job.

They are thinking of entering into a postnuptial agreement that will somehow assure Melissa that Elliot's new business venture won't interfere with the financial security they have built up during the marriage. She is understandably concerned about there being adequate financial resources for their current living expenses and eventual retirement and old age. The challenge of figuring out this postnup is how accommodate the aims of both parties, and how to be fair to both if the new business fails.

The new venture may require so much money that if the business does go under, the couple will be left with a financially challenged retirement (if they can retire at all). Potentially facing an impoverished old age is a serious situation for both spouses to consider when making the decision about a new business venture. It's a decision they need to make together, with much reflection. When one spouse makes that decision alone, it is often a recipe for marital disaster.

If the business fails, will there be any money to protect the non-business spouse? Will there be enough money to protect *both* spouses? They are *both* entitled to protection and security in a long-term marriage. Is it fair to just charge the business spouse for the loss if the business fails? This would be done by subtracting the business loss from a marital settlement if there is a divorce. Is it fair to the business spouse for the other enjoy and accept the fruits of the business if it is a success but not it if fails? The implications of leaving the risk of loss totally on the business spouse need to be carefully considered. The view must consider the long term: What might be the repercussions during the next ten, twenty, or thirty years of the marriage?

Another situation that can lead people toward wanting to have a postnup is this: One spouse is about to receive, or has received, an inheritance from their parents. Maybe that spouse feels like the other partner didn't achieve the level of financial success that was hoped for at the start of the marriage. Maybe that spouse feels it's fair to have the inheritance stay within the bloodlines. Or maybe that spouse's parents had expressed an intention to have the legacy stay with their children and grandchildren. Maybe the marriage is currently at a less-than-contented stage. This may drive the party expecting the inheritance to want to protect it as their own.

State laws generally provide that inherited money is deemed to be the separate property of the recipient, unless it's commingled with marital property or used to support the family.

But what if there is not enough marital property in the marriage to adequately support both spouses as they age? What if the inheritance means that one party can take vacations and the other must remain working into their late 70s? What if the couple made living expense decisions based on the fact that one of them would receive an inheritance from their parents?

What if they assumed that this inheritance would fund the retirement of both of them and they made employment and career decisions based on that during their marriage? You can see there are many painful decisions to be made when considering this situation and formulating the terms that might apply to it in a postnup. The terms of a postnup should reflect the increasing obligations that spouses have toward each other as the marriage grows longer.

Another example would be a couple that wishes to have a postnup to guarantee that certain estate-planning actions are taken if their marriage ends with the death of their spouse.

Some people enter second marriages without adequate thought of how they would balance financial allegiance to their new spouse with the financial allegiance to their children of a previous marriage. This can be a point of contention that develops over time in the new marriage. A thoughtful postnup process can be very helpful toward finding a pathway to navigate these parallel loyalties. The couple can establish mutually contemplated and agreed-to estate plan terms in the postnup, and then fulfill the terms by seeking an estate-planning attorney and executing the appropriate estate-planning documents.

Or perhaps, like many second marriages, the issue of inheritance for and from *each other,* if the marriage ends in death, was left open when they signed the agreement, as is (unfortunately) often the case. (See Chapter 9 about the importance of having a mutual inheritance requirement.) The spouses now want to make sure that they are contractually obligated to follow through on the estate plan they have decided upon for everyone's mutual protection and peace of mind. The terms can be set in the postnup and be followed up by signing the actual estate-planning documents, if not already done.

Occasionally, a postnuptial agreement is sought because the spouses went through a harsh and upsetting prenuptial agreement process in the negotiations and interactions with opposing counsels. It ended up in a painful signing close to the wedding. Often parties report that their attorneys did not do what they asked them to do when the prenup was negotiated and drafted. It's good to find new attorneys that are more sensitive to the needs and wishes of the couple. (See Chapter 20.) A postnuptial agreement (especially when created with a mediator's help) can do much to undo the harm that resulted from the earlier toxic negotiations and the resulting bitter agreement.

Often the negotiation and signing of a prenup before a marriage is hurried, leaving both parties dissatisfied and putting a damper on the joy of the wedding. Letting some time elapse before deciding to get a postnup is good, even a year or more after the wedding. This hiatus can give people time to process what they might have done differently had they had more time. A couple's thoughts about some of the terms of their prenup are likely to have changed or been more fully thought out since they married.

Maybe they had children. Maybe they're more relaxed about sharing and more trusting of each other. Maybe they're more optimistic about the strength of their marriage, having spent more time together. These parties can come back and decide on the terms they really want now that will align much more closely with how they view things after being married for a while. They may even decide to terminate or cancel their prenuptial agreement.

Some prenups have trigger dates for vesting of separate property and income into marital property. As the trigger dates approach, people start obsessing about the health of their marriage. They may be questioning whether their marriage is good enough to continue. Sometimes couples want to change or omit the trigger dates because of these feelings and the disturbance occurring within their marriage as these dates approached. (See Chapter 19 for discussion of the benefits of monthly vesting schedules.)

Sometimes there has been an infidelity issue that a spouse wants to address in a postnup. One party may have strayed in the marriage and had an affair. Or the parties may decide to put a clause in a postnup to punish a party who has started drinking, using drugs, or gambling. There may be a financial penalty clause in the postnup if the bad behavior reoccurs. These are called "lifestyle" or "bad-boy, bad-girl" postnups.

The problem with these postnup terms is that enforceability becomes an issue. The infidelity clauses are a problem for courts to enforce. Courts and judges do not wish to enter the bedrooms of litigants. A financial penalty for the breacher may not be enforceable in the subsequent divorce case. This postnup term might well be invalidated.

The theory of postnuptial agreements is that they are supposed to help maintain and improve a marriage and not be a substitute for a divorce agreement. In other words, postnups are supposed to *prevent* divorce, not *increase* the chances of divorce. Because the idea of a postnup often arises when a marriage is already failing, postnups may "encourage" divorce because they provide a ready-made exit plan or a way to benefit a party in a future divorce.

The difference between encouraging and preventing divorce turns out to be a very fine line to navigate, which is why many courts are leery about postnups. But if needed and handled sensitively, a postnuptial agreement can be a very effective tool in some cases to help a marriage to continue and hopefully improve.

Marital counseling or couples therapy is often a good first step for people wanting to change the personal or financial framework of their marriage. Another possibility for a couple considering a postnup is to seek help from a marital mediator. Marital mediation is a relatively new form of mediation. It is focused on the present, not the past. It tends to have a practical outlook. Some spouses prefer it over marital counseling.

It is helpful that the marital mediator be a practicing attorney and have the same skill set as a prenuptial agreement lawyer or mediator. That person will be a neutral mediator who assists a couple to identify and discuss financial issues and communication problems that may be causing the marriage to be troubled. The process may or may not end up with the couple wanting to enter into a written postnuptial agreement. Often the mediation process can help a couple come to an understanding of the causes of their distress and assist them in finding solutions. If both spouses truly want to stay together, marital mediation is a process that can help them achieve that goal, whether or not it results in a written postnuptial agreement.

People in marriages should be very cautious about entering into (or thinking about) postnups. They are not a magic pill that can solve all marital problems. Courts have called them "innately coercive" because often an ultimatum is involved. What if a business-owner spouse told his wife that he would divorce her unless he retained sole ownership of the business that he had developed during the marriage? What if one spouse told the other that they would divorce them unless they made the inheritance their spouse had just received marital property? Would a postnup serve these couples well?

This is why many courts posit that a "cloak of protection" should be thrown over postnuptial agreements to make sure they are arrived at "fairly and equitably." A court may set aside or refuse to enforce a postnup that is "born of and subsisting in inequity" or that is so one-sided as to be "manifestly unfair."

Practitioners engaged in drafting, negotiating, or mediating post-nups need to be mindful as to whether a postnup they are working on is meant to extend and improve a marriage or whether it is being negotiated by one party to gain advantage in an imminent divorce. Valuable consideration (such as rights conferred) mutually given and received by each of the spouses (other than the mere continuation of the marriage) may demonstrate fair play and take it out of the zone of questionable validity.

CHAPTER 19:

HOW TO MAKE
BOTH PARTIES HAPPY

Throughout this book, I've discussed the many drawbacks to having a prenup. The flip side of this is that there is a path toward finding solutions to these drawbacks when a prenup is needed. Discovering what can make a prenup satisfactory to *both* parties is a core message of this book. That is not to say that everyone should have a prenup. There are very good reasons not to, as most marrying couples come to decide.

First, people need to remember that a prenuptial agreement is an *agreement*. That means the parties to the contract should actually *agree*. But that generally doesn't happen with prenups. The usual case (at least in first marriages) is that one party wants a prenup and the other party doesn't. If the parties don't agree and the contract is signed anyway, it will likely be an enforceable prenup, but it won't necessarily be a good prenup.

If one party doesn't want the prenup, the problems begin. That party, and their attorney, will want to advocate for better terms to protect their client's interests. Often the resistance (usually by the attorney for the more-moneyed fiancé) is fierce.

Think about the various techniques described in this book that can meet both parties' need for fairness and security. These can be used to meet the more-moneyed spouse's desire for protection and fairness, and at the same time they can provide an equitable and secure result to the less-moneyed spouse. Ask your attorneys to build these provisions into the first draft of the prenup.

If you are the less-moneyed spouse and are faced with the prospect of a prenup, encourage your fiancé to start the process with mediation. A term sheet generated through multiple face-to-face, three-way meetings with the assistance of a neutral facilitator is the optimum way to begin the process. (See Chapter 21.) Using this process, you can mutually decide upon the terms that feel good to both of you.

If you are not starting with the mediation process, you can share with your fiancé options that your attorney described to you (or that you found in this book) that may be more conducive to supporting the marriage. Talking together with your future spouse *before* any draft is generated by the attorneys may help prevent the angst of receiving a draft with features that alienate the person you love. Beginning with a term sheet that you and your future spouse can adjust with your attorneys (or mediator) rather than a full-blown prenup sent by the more-moneyed spouse's attorney is a good way to start.

If there is a lot of conflict during the process, it is often a good idea for the two of you to see a therapist or marital counselor together. It's best to find a therapist who is experienced with divorce, finances, and family issues. A good way to find one would be by searching your statewide collaborative law organization or local collaborative law practice groups. Therapists with this type of sensitivity and experience will be listed under coach, facilitator, or neutral-process coach in the collaborative law organization's website. Remember, since most sessions would be conducted via Zoom, geographical location is not important.

An important question to have answered is, "What does consideration have to do with it?" The short answer is a lot! "Consideration," as a legal concept, plays into contract law. The requirements of this legal contract are that there must be mutual assent, consideration, and capacity to contract. The last requirement should be easy to meet for most people getting married. But what about mutual assent and consideration?

Acquiring mutual assent is one of the core problems with prenups if one party really doesn't want one. Assent might be given unwillingly by one of the parties. But, almost always, this does not rise to the level where one could say the assent was "coerced" or the contract was written under duress, which would make the contract legally unenforceable.

There is also the question of consideration. Normally, a contract needs to be supported by consideration. There is a trade of value in which each party gives the other something of equal value. But with prenups, that does not seem to be the usual requirement. Legal rights are taken away, and often nothing or little is given in exchange. The sense of the word "consideration" as having regard for the needs for one another is missing. (See Chapter 10). This especially stings at the beginning of a marriage. It's not hard to see how this might be damaging to the loving relationship.

But it doesn't have to be that way. Equal trades *can* be made. Rights to property under state law that are conferred to the more-moneyed spouse can be relinquished or softened while still meeting that party's particular goals. Rights that are important to the less-moneyed spouse that are better than what might be provided under state laws can be conferred. That kind of parity is what you can find when you are embarking on a prenup.

Here are some actions you can take in the terms of your prenup to make this happen:

You can build in a significant gift at the time of the marriage. Putting your house (which you both will live in) in joint names at the outset or having a plan to do so soon after the wedding may be a good thing. Commit to funding and creating an asset account in joint names. Pay off your future spouse's debt. If you are considering a prenup, you probably have enough money to be generous and to part with some of it. It's a perfect way of showing you believe in your upcoming marriage and want to give something to your future spouse, and not just take something away.

A healthy paradigm for first marriages is to share all income earned by both spouses, no matter what the difference in that income might be. This would include income from employment, bonuses, stock options, restricted stock, and other employee incentives. Self-employment income and profits of active business interests also should be shared. Shared marital income would also include additions to retirement accounts and profit sharing during the marriage, including any employer contributions. This is all consistent with state law. There's nothing wrong with having large swaths of your prenup consistent with state law. State laws on divorce are not an enemy. They should be persuasive.

For purposes of the prenup, it shouldn't matter whether this earned income is held in separate or joint accounts. It would be deemed a marital asset however it is held. But surprisingly, some standard "off-the-shelf" prenups state that even earned income during the marriage is not necessarily a marital asset unless it is put into a joint account. This sort of language gives one party to the prenup too much control in deciding what is separate and what is marital. It can cause resentment and hoarding. (See Chapter 8.)

Many people with prenups have parents who make lifetime gifts to them. People like to help their children get a "leg up" in life. Some of these gifts are annual exclusion gifts under Internal Revenue Code section 2503(b), currently $18,000 a year. (Contrary to widespread belief, this does *not* mean that the gifts must be limited to that amount.) Many parents confer larger gifts to their adult children to help them get established when they need it, not when the parents have died.

You could stipulate in the prenup that any of these gifts from parents during marriage are marital property, no matter to whom the gift is made. Or you could have a rule stating that any gift in a year to either spouse under $50,000 (or some other number) is marital. That same rule could be applied to gifts that are received as distributions from family trusts.

Living in a house you own jointly is important to most married couples. In legal parlance this is called a "marital residence." It has great emotional meaning to most married people. When a home is owned only by one of the spouses, the non-owning spouse can feel disconnected from it. In a fundamental way, it doesn't feel to that spouse that it is their home. It creates a separateness that can weaken the marriage. Having a plan to achieve joint ownership is a good step. Or if one spouse wishes to keep sole ownership of a property, perhaps it would be better for the marriage to buy another house together to live in and hold jointly, and for the owner-spouse to rent out their former house.

Sometimes wealthy parents want to make a financial contribution to the purchase of a home for their children but want to make sure that this gift of funds doesn't become marital property in the event of a divorce. Or the parents may buy the house but put it in a trust that will never benefit the less-moneyed spouse if there is a divorce or even if the marriage ends in the death of the more-moneyed spouse.

Overall, it might be better for newlyweds to forgo this type of assistance and for the couple to do it on their own. This may mean the purchase of a less expensive house and the need to take out a mortgage. You may be better off to look a gift horse in the mouth and say "no" when it comes to accepting parental help when purchasing a marital residence, unless it comes without strings.

Prenups can have provisions that vest separate property into marital property gradually. It's a very good way to soften some of the harshness of prenups and provide some consideration to a less-moneyed spouse. With vesting clauses, you can customize what and when you will be sharing. The vesting can increase over time, thus reflecting the longevity and stability of the marriage.

There are many options for vesting. You can vest income from separate assets and/or the separate assets themselves. Or you can use the "snapshot" method. Under that method, you can vest the gain in the value of separate property, but you keep ownership of the principal with the party who owned it at the time of the marriage. You would value the assets as of the date of marriage. This may be established using the financial statements attached to the prenup. Then you could provide that all increases of assets beyond that point on both sides of the equation (i.e., both spouses' assets) are marital. That means that increases in the value of securities, as well as interest, dividends accumulated in the accounts, are marital. This is a very simple way of vesting and keeping track.

Be aware that there are tax implications in vesting, so you will need to make sure that tax is allocated fairly between separate property and marital property. Prenup tax provision clauses can be drafted to address and resolve this issue.

Vesting doesn't have to be an all-or-nothing proposition. You can also vest just a percentage of the income or gain, and/or a percentage of principal of the assets. Or you can give the owner of the separate property some return on principal (using a published interest rate, a specific market rate, or one tied to the Consumer Price Index) and vest the rest into marital property. The possibilities are really limitless.

You can structure a vesting schedule to begin at a certain point or year in the marriage that will gradually get to 100 percent or some other percentage. (At 100 percent vested, the vested property will be owned 50 percent by each spouse.) That vesting schedule may be applied to all or part of the value of an asset. The original owner-spouse would continue to own a share of their assets held prior to marriage, which could be more than 50 percent to reflect the origin of the assets. The vesting could apply to only certain assets, and not others, for more flexibility.

There can be straight-line vesting with the same percentage of vested assets each year. It can start at the date of marriage or at some later date or anniversary. I've also seen vesting where the percentages start out at a smaller percentage and increase over time as the marriage proves itself to be durable.

For vesting schedules, many choose trigger anniversaries. I think monthly vesting accruals are preferable. They can be articulated simply in the prenup. If you have major vesting points at certain anniversary dates of the marriage (e.g., at five, ten, twenty years), these trigger dates can put a lot of pressure on the marital relationship at those times.

For instance, if there is a jump in vesting percentages at five years or ten years or fifteen years, the more-moneyed spouse might start ruminating about the financial ramifications of continuing the marriage before that trigger date deadline. They may start obsessing about whether the marriage is good enough to continue, given the financial changes that will take place at that trigger point. These are thoughts that they wouldn't necessarily have if there were monthly vesting. Also, the couple might have totally forgotten about the prenup until the vesting dates come up. But now they remember, and if they had a bad experience negotiating the prenup, all those negative feelings will come flooding back at the trigger date.

State laws generally provide that premarital property, as well as gains and earnings on premarital property, are separate property. However, if one future spouse has plentiful assets and the other doesn't, vesting is a way to even up the situation. The abundance is shared with the spouse while still giving the wealthier spouse whatever you decide reflects the origin of the money, plus half the marital assets that had been vested. Sharing tends to be good for a marriage. It's not rocket science.

It is especially important to look at the situation where one of the spouses has enough assets to never work again, due to family wealth, the sale of a business, or retirement after a successful business career. This often comes up in a second marriage where the other future spouse still needs to accumulate adequate security for their retirement and old age. Even though legally the more-moneyed spouse's premarital property is "separate property," something needs to be done to protect the less-moneyed spouse's future. This can and should be planned for when determining the features of your prenup.

Most prenups provide that if a spouse contributes separate property into marital property, they have the right to track it as separate property, and they even have a right to a percentage of gain attributable to their percentage of contribution. The presumption that any such contribution becomes marital unless otherwise agreed to by the parties can be a good provision to include in a prenup. It makes the probability of a generous gift into the marital estate by a more-moneyed spouse more likely.

How income from a closely held business will be treated is very important to address in a prenup if one of the spouses is an active participant in the business. Their efforts in the business are marital efforts according to the laws of every state. Business income (including profits) and any increase in value of the business efforts of the spouse are generally marital under state law. It's important that the efforts (including financial ones) put forth by each of the spouses be shared for the sake of the marriage. Defining what is the income or growth of the business due to a spouse's efforts can be challenging but must be addressed when formulating the terms of a prenup. (See Chapter 14 for more detail.)

Consider what happens when a person leaves the geographical area where they are living and/or working to marry someone. It happens quite frequently, and it can be a big financial risk for the party who is relocating and perhaps changing their job. This is similar to when a spouse leaves the workforce or puts their career on hold to have children and build a family.

When someone moves to a new location to marry, a provision in a prenup might be a monetary settlement for the relocating party to start over again, either in the city in which they lived previously or the place where that party relocated, should the marriage fail. In legal language, that's called "making the injured party whole." The settlement can vary, depending on how long after the marriage a divorce occurs.

It's hard to look into the future to determine a loss before the fact, so arbitration can be the method of choice to determine the amount or mode of remedy for these situations. Using a conflict resolution option can create a fair reimbursement for spouses who have changed their positions to marry. This may be necessary to get them back on their feet, as it were, and to make them whole again.

Something else to consider is the potential for inheritance from the parents of the marrying couple. Prenups usually categorize any inheritance as "separate property" of the heir. A prenup can address this issue in a few ways. Some people might want to have all inheritances remain separate; some decide to vest it all as marital property upon the death of all the couple's parents. At this point, the couple usually is in a long-term marriage. Even though the inheritances may not be of equal value, it may well be more beneficial to the marriage to consider these assets as marital.

A possible wrinkle in this plan would be if the parents put the inheritance into a trust. This is common in estate planning among wealthy parents. In this case, you would need to address what income or principal might be expected to come from the trust over time. (Look at the trust instrument and its terms for those specifics.) Then, how do you treat the money coming out of the trust? A good option would be to share any funds that that are distributed from the trusts. Remember that keeping separate property tends to "separate" a couple.

You hear a lot about "sunset clauses" in prenups. These are clauses that state, "After X years, this prenup will be terminated and shall be null and void and have no further effect." While this may seem attractive, sunset clauses in prenups do come with some downsides.

One of the things that might disappear would be an inheritance protection provision. In state law, inheritance protections for spouses are often less robust than what the typical first marriage estate plan would provide and may be even less than what the prenup prescribed. So, you'd lose this protection if you have a sunset clause.

Often prenups have other provisions for a less-moneyed spouse that are more robust than what would be required under state laws, such as vesting of premarital or inherited property. Another protection that would be lost is the Alternative Dispute Resolution (ADR) clause that many prenups contain. Having this clause lays the groundwork for a civilized out-of-court route if the marriage ends in divorce or if there's a dispute between a surviving spouse and the heirs, executors, trustees, etc. of the deceased spouse.

Another issue to consider is the potential impact of the looming sunset clause trigger date. This is like the trigger dates set up by other vesting schedule dates. It can cause the couple to "rethink" the state of the success of their marriage. So carefully consider the pros and cons of putting a sunset clause in your prenup and pay heed to which provisions it might apply to.

CHAPTER 20:

HOW TO FIND A GOOD PRENUP ATTORNEY

One of the most important decisions you will make during the process of getting a prenup is choosing your attorney. We attorneys are not all the same. We have different personalities and values. Our philosophies about marriage, divorce, and prenuptial agreements vary quite a bit. Our personal life experiences play a large part in the advice we give our clients. The task of finding an attorney to represent you on your journey toward a prenup should include finding someone who can guide you in an appropriate way and who can respond to your views and concerns about all things prenup — including whether or not you really need one.

A good prenup attorney is one who can be creative about the possibilities that are available to you. That attorney should be able to think "outside of the box" and treat every prenup anew. A prenup attorney should be sensitive to the dynamics of marriage.

In my experience, every prenup is different, requiring a different approach to its formulation to effectively create the financial terms of the upcoming marriage. In the field of prenuptial agreements, many attorneys have a fixed view of what a prenup should say and what the terms should be. Because each couple is unique, the "one-size-fits-all" view is likely not right for you. Attorneys who choose the same stock prenup formula with the usual terms without much customization to your individual situations and wishes may not serve you well.

Your prenup attorney should not just be a "yes" man or woman. They should listen to you, but they also should give you honest feedback as to the terms you might want to propose. That's where the attorney's view of marriage might come into play.

Suppose you want to share premarital property with your new spouse? Your attorney should tell you what "the law" is — that in most cases premarital property is the separate property of the person who owns it. But if the attorney tries to persuade you to keep your property separate after you marry, then that attorney is not reflecting your wishes as to how to structure the financial terms of your marriage. They are reflecting their own view, that protection of your premarital assets should be of paramount value for you in your marriage.

Sometimes an attorney might put a certain provision into a prenup, even when requested by a client not to do so. Or the attorney may have failed to put in a provision that you wanted because the attorney disagreed with you. This causes a lot of unnecessary stress in the negotiations and often great distress for the other future spouse because they might think this provision (which might be very adverse for them) was something that *you* wanted. I have seen this happen in many cases. It's not pretty. It's hard to recover from something like that.

The attorney you choose should be sensitive to the dynamics of marriage, and probably should either be in a long-term marriage or have experienced one. For a prenup, your attorney should be mature. I prefer to refer people to someone over 55 years old and with at least 20 years of experience as an attorney. A younger attorney is less experienced and may not have been in a long-term marital relationship yet.

Your attorney should be able to explain the legal aspects of the contract in plain English, not legalese. They should explain your state's rules applying to married people in divorce, marriage, and death, so that you understand what rights you might be waiving in the prenup or what you are receiving in the contract that might be better for you than state law would require. A less-moneyed spouse should not be endlessly punished by taking away their rights. Prenups can and should give important rights to that spouse, too. Some prenup lawyers don't think so.

Signing a prenup, for most people, is the most financially significant contract they will ever execute, much more significant, for instance, than buying a house. So, it's best that your primary goal not be to save money on legal fees. If you're a person who really needs a prenup, you probably have enough money to pay for a professional work product. Looking for a "flat fee" attorney may not serve you well, as it is likely you will be engaging an attorney who is not very experienced, and perhaps quite young. And at that low price, the prenup will not be customized and the attorney-client discussions, which take time and attention, will be curtailed.

Don't try to do it yourself with fillable forms you might access online. If you use a website to construct a prenup and don't use an attorney, you could well miss important issues on which an attorney could advise you. Not having the best professional-quality work on your prenup is like trying to remove your own appendix. And although you might save money in the short run, you may lose a great deal of money when the prenup comes into play (which it *will*) either at divorce or death.

Hiring a capable, experienced attorney who will give you sound advice about the terms of your prenup as you develop it is critical to the process and the result. And the result is important: Will your marriage be improved and sustained by the prenup, or will it be weakened due to resulting financial conflict?

Many times, clients come to me after talking together about what their prenup's terms should be. They think that talking about it is the best first step. But there are problems in not getting counsel from an attorney (or mediator) near the beginning of the process.

First, the couple hasn't received advice about what the law provides. They may be creating their "own law" without fully understanding the benefits of what the *existing* law says. Second, they may not understand what is involved in a long-term marriage.

Contrary to what prenup ads say ("when you marry, you already have a prenup"), that is not necessarily a bad thing. The "law" isn't the enemy. State marriage laws are well reasoned and constructed. When you are structuring your prenup, you will benefit from an awareness of the valuable marriage-related concepts imbedded in the "law" that people in long (and short) marriages find important. Making up your own law in a prenup in a vacuum without knowing the possibilities and understanding the implications of what is already out there is problematic.

Then there's the problem of inequality in assets and income. The less-moneyed spouse will usually defer to the wishes of the more-moneyed spouse, feeling that they don't deserve to share in the wealth. That's a problem an experienced attorney can help guide people through.

There are several interrelated areas of law that are important to know if you are a prenuptial agreement attorney. They are divorce law, probate law, estate planning, business law, elder law, tax law, and, of course, the law of prenuptial agreements. As a result, your attorney probably should be a generalist, practicing in or at least knowing about each of these areas. This broad knowledge base is like that of a primary care physician or an internal medicine physician.

There are three major legal fields that attorneys who provide prenup representation come from. They are estate-planning lawyers, business lawyers, and divorce lawyers. Each tends to have different points of view as to what a prenup should achieve. Estate planners and business attorneys tend to represent more-moneyed spouses. Their primary aim tends to be financial risk control for the more-moneyed spouse, without thinking about the risk the prenup terms may bring to the marriage itself. Often, they do not focus on what rights the other spouse might relinquish and the effect that this might have on the health of the marriage.

I find that divorce attorneys are much more sensitive to the dynamics of marriage — what makes them work and what makes them fail — than other types of lawyers. My sense is that they are more able to balance risk control with provisions that can lead to sharing and positive financial behavior that nurtures married couples. Also, since much of the work in formulating a prenuptial agreement concerns what happens if the parties divorce, divorce lawyers know the laws pertaining to every aspect of marriage and divorce. They understand the reasons for the laws that are imbedded in statutes and case rulings. This can be very helpful to a client who is formulating a prenup. Estate-planning attorneys and business attorneys can be consulted in prenup cases when needed.

My view on prenups (perhaps a minority view) is that they are not solely documents for the purpose of asset or risk protection, as some attorneys view them. They are that; but they also should create a reasonable financial structure for a marriage. The protections should apply to both future spouses. Benefits should be given to both spouses, not just one. They should not be one-sided. I call a prenup a "financial plan for your marriage" because that's what it is at its essence. Make it a good plan for both of you.

Marriage is a special relationship that is very different from that of unrelated parties negotiating a business contract. The prenup should reflect this special relationship. If a prenup is sound, it should result in both parties feeling good about it as they enter the marriage.

It is usually not helpful to engage the family attorney of one of the future spouses. That "family" attorney will follow the marching orders of the more-wealthy spouse's parents. Otherwise, that attorney would lose a very important client: the parents. This can pose an inherent conflict of interest, where the attorney may not be representing the future spouse's best interests, but promoting the parents' wishes.

Sometimes, when the prenup is required by the wealthy parents, their child may accept the family attorney as his or her attorney to create peace in the family. But it *does* come with potential costs to the future spouses, unless the legitimate interests of the future spouses are respected, reflected, and put into effect.

Personal referrals are another way that people often try to find prenuptial agreement attorneys. The problem with this is that often the recommended attorney may not be a prenuptial agreement attorney. Or they may not be the *right* prenup attorney for you.

A good screening method is to avoid considering litigation attorneys for your counsel. In general, they have less of a cooperative mindset and tend to be adversarial. Stay away from lawyers whose ads refer to them as a "high-energy" or "zealous," or a relentless advocate." A lawyer who presents themselves as this may not benefit the process. It's not fun to have attorneys battling it out when you and your future spouse love each other and are trying to get married. Having this type of attorney may make the negotiations more negative than either of you want them to be. You're getting married, and you won't want to get into an adversarial process with your future spouse.

A good source of referrals may be an attorney who has already been engaged by one of the future spouses. In this case, usually the two attorneys have a good history of working together on cases. They are likely to be compatible and trust each other to be fair and reasonable.

However, there is a danger in this option. Say, for instance, one of the attorneys (usually the one for the more-moneyed spouse) makes a referral to another lawyer to represent the other party. If that other lawyer advocates too hard to assert rights for their client, they may never get another referral from that attorney going forward. It's a real problem.

I have found that, in general, the best prenuptial attorneys are "collaborative divorce" attorneys. When working with prenup clients as mediator, these are the attorneys I choose from in creating a referral list. Collaborative law has been around for about 35 years. It's becoming more widely practiced. There are now collaborative lawyers in every state, and most states have collaborative law associations and practice groups. Although collaborative law is mostly practiced in divorce law, there are also business law, civil law, and elder law collaborative law practitioners.

"Collaborative divorce" is a coordinated process involving the two divorce clients and their two attorneys. There are a series of four-way meetings to resolve the terms of the divorce. Usually there's also a fifth person at the meetings, a neutral process coach who keeps the discussion positive. The neutral process coach is generally someone credentialed as a psychologist or family therapist.

The process is like co-mediation, but with counsel advice, strategy, and advocacy occurring between meetings in the individual sessions with the attorneys and their clients. During the meetings, there is every attempt to be, yes, *collaborative*, attempting to work constructively together toward the goals: fair, just, and workable terms for the upcoming divorce.

It works beautifully in complex divorce cases and tends to preserve family relationships. The peacefulness of the process greatly benefits the children of divorce. Collaborative lawyers are usually trained in divorce mediation, which benefits the process. As you may sense, a collaborative divorce lawyer can be an excellent choice for a prenup lawyer. I have definitely found it to be so, and in my work, it has been an effective screening process for my clients.

Part of my practice, when I'm a mediator for prenup clients, is to find suitable attorneys to represent my mediation clients. I have come to the point where I search only for collaborative divorce attorneys when I create the list of potential attorneys. In the prenup context, you would not engage in a formal collaborative law process with five-way meetings of the clients, attorneys, and neutral process coach. That would almost always be unnecessary and burdensome. Rather, this quality of representation, especially if you both engage collaborative lawyers, will maximize the chance of having a more harmonious prenup process than is typical when two noncollaborative attorneys are involved.

When the two attorneys representing you are collaborative lawyers, there is a different feel to the entire process. Concerns and options are discussed and thought through. There is good communication between the two attorneys. The process is gentler and more compassionate. The prenup can become a vehicle that offers something for each future spouse and is not just a zero-sum game, where things are withdrawn from one spouse for the benefit of the other.

To find collaborative divorce attorneys in your state, use Google to search for practitioners. in your state by employing this search string:

[your state] collaborative divorce attorney mediation prenuptial

It's good to include the word "mediation" in the search string to pull in attorneys for whom alternative dispute resolution (ADR), and not litigation, is a central part of their practice and view of law.

You can find statewide collaborative organizations and practice groups of collaborative attorneys using this search string:

[your state] collaborative divorce

The organizations and practice groups usually show up before the attorneys. The organization websites will list collaborative attorneys and give their profiles and a link to the attorney's website. You can search their bios and get more information about that attorney from their own websites.

When considering a prenup where there are irrevocable trusts created by parents or grandparents, try to find a collaborative attorney who also works in the field of estate planning. If one of you is actively engaged in a business, it might be helpful to find a collaborative attorney who practices in business law, in addition to divorce.

When evaluating an attorney that your search discovers, take a look at what they say about themselves in their bios. Do they emphasize out-of-court solutions to divorce cases? Have they personally written their bios or is it a "canned" bio? Is it a personally written website or a "canned" one, merely optimized for SEO. Do they belong to any collaborative law or mediation associations in their states? Have they assumed leadership roles in any of these organizations?

And then there's that undefinable reaction you get from just looking at their photo and seeing how they present themselves as a lawyer and person. Don't discount that. Your sense of them when looking at their headshot may be a good indication of someone you might feel comfortable working with on this tender project.

Remember, attorneys can make or break prenups. Choose carefully.

CHAPTER 21:

WHY MEDIATION IS USUALLY THE BEST FIRST STEP

As discussed in previous chapters, it is generally (really, always) difficult for a couple to talk about the potential terms of a prenup face-to-face. There is often a perceived power imbalance when there is a disparity in wealth or earning capacity. The discussion seems to stray from the original commitment to share in a marriage. This makes both parties feel badly. The more-moneyed spouse feels guilty when they ask the other to give up marital rights and make concessions. It's not an easy situation. The less-moneyed spouse feels sad, perhaps mistreated, and perhaps feels that they don't deserve to share in the other's earning capacity or family wealth.

The couple also doesn't have an adequate "toolbox" to work with. This is the information about what options are possible in the prenup that an experienced prenup mediator (usually an attorney with a background in divorce law) can share with the couple. The mediator also facilitates clear and open communication when discussing topics in a prenup.

Neutral facilitation of difficult conversations creates a safe place for the couple to start talking about what the financial plan for the marriage will and should be. Without a neutral, knowledgeable facilitator making it an open three-way discussion, the discussion of prenup terms between the future spouses can get very "hot." It becomes argumentative, accusatorial, and unproductive. It causes harm to their relationship and infects their feelings toward each other. Almost everyone negotiating a prenup face-to-face has had that experience.

Going directly to an attorney to get the process started (and skipping the mediation process) is generally not a good idea. Usually, the first draft comes from the attorney for the more-moneyed spouse-to-be. It is often one-sided, in favor of that spouse, to the detriment of the other. It's a positional beginning that takes a toll on the relationship between the couple. It's bound to create waves of unhappiness and anxiety for all involved. It's almost always extremely upsetting to the couple.

It's better to take a deep breath and step back. The best first step should be to create a term sheet, which is a simple list of the basic terms that the couple thinks should be in the prenup. And the best way to do this is in a series of discussions facilitated by a trained and experienced prenuptial agreement mediator. That way the couple will have the benefit of the knowledge and experience of the mediator and not get into hot, unproductive discussions. The mediation process can lead toward actual agreement of the terms that will be incorporated in the final document.

In the prenup process, each spouse should be represented by a separate attorney. If the couple starts with a mediated term sheet, the attorneys may be engaged after the term sheet is constructed. Sometimes the attorneys enter the picture earlier and are in the "wings" giving advice to their clients as the process unfolds. There will probably be mutually agreed-upon adjustments as advice is filtered down by the clients' attorneys. Attorneys can improve and fine-tune the agreements made in mediation. The attorneys are the ones who generally draft the actual agreement incorporating the terms.

Sometimes clients enter mediation after having had a very negative and hurtful process handled by their two separate attorneys. Many of my clients come to me after this experience had almost driven them apart. Working with a mediator can be helpful for starting all over and cleaning the slate. This occurs after the clients have stopped working with their initial attorneys.

When I'm called upon to work with a couple in this situation, we start anew. I always suggest that the clients engage new counsel to serve as their reviewing attorneys once the mediation is concluded. If I look at the work product that the prior attorney-led fiasco came up with, it tends to be much later in the process. The situation for the clients was so toxic that they don't want to re-experience it by looking at that work product. Part of my process is to help the couple find appropriate attorneys to represent them. (See Chapter 20.)

At the first meeting with the couple, the mediator should become familiar with each of the parties' factual situations. How long have they been together? What is their sense of the marriage? Is it a first or second marriage? Are there children from the first marriage? Are either of their sets of parents divorced? If the clients themselves have been divorced, what was their experience? Have they been struggling over having a prenup or the terms they want in it? Have they had a bad experience with attorneys that have previously represented them in connection with the prenup?

A good mediator should also find out what the clients' plans are. Do they expect to have children? At what point? Do they expect to have more than one child? Do either of them expect the mother or the father to leave the job market? If so, for how long? If it's a second marriage, how do they plan to provide legacies for the children of the first marriage? How do they envision providing for their own and their spouse's needs as they age? What type of financial plan do they want to set up in their "gray" prenup?

It's important to become intimately knowledgeable about the

mediation clients' background and their plans and expectations. Short-circuiting this by going straight to the financial provisions is a mistake. There are many essential background issues to discuss and fully understand first.

Also, during these initial fact-finding sessions, the couple and the mediator are getting to know each other. The mediator starts to understand the dynamics between the clients and their particular communication style. Evidence of misunderstandings and miscommunications between the couple quickly becomes apparent to a mediator. This is because mediators tend to be experts in analyzing communication issues. As a neutral third party, the mediator can (gently) point out when these difficulties occur. This alone relieves the clients of the many "negative tapes" they are developing about each other based on the struggles they are having about the terms of the prenup.

In mediation, the clients have a safe place to air their views on all the substantive issues germane to the prenup. If someone is concerned about how to handle receiving a potential inheritance, the mediator can encourage the parties to fully discuss it and brainstorm toward solutions. If someone is concerned about their concept of sharing in a marriage, it can be aired out fully and all options laid out and discussed. It's good to take the discussions slowly and space out the mediation sessions so that all three parties (future spouses and mediator) can ponder them between sessions. The process should not be short-circuited.

How will the couple handle premarital property? Will it belong solely to the person who owns it for the entirety of the marriage? Will the income and gain from it also belong solely to that person? That's usually what state law provides. But in a prenup, you are "making your own law." So, all the different ways of handling premarital property can be laid out by the mediator. They can then be openly discussed and adopted or not. But at least there will have been an opportunity for an open, facilitated discussion. The issue won't have been swept under the rug or presented as a *fait accompli* in the prenup draft presented by the attorney for the more-moneyed spouse.

What if it's something I call a "mixed marriage"? That's when one future spouse comes from a wealthy family and the other comes from a middle-class or working-class family. This is a frequent fact pattern with couples I work with. There will need to be discussions of what happens when the family wealth is transferred to one of the spouses, and also when it passes to their children and grandchildren. These are important discussions to have.

If there are irrevocable trusts involved (such as generation-skipping trusts or dynasty trusts), they need to be looked at and understood by both future spouses. A mediator with knowledge of trusts and estate planning can explain the significance of the terms and the effect on their marriage with both future spouses. I have found that screen-sharing the trust document in real time with the couple can be a game-changer. Often the future spouse who is the beneficiary of the trust had not really understood its terms. Knowledge is so important because the trust exists and can't be ignored. So having a full understanding of the terms they include and a discussion of how it will affect the marriage is crucial.

What if one of the future spouses has significant student debt? This is quite common. Almost universally, a prenup coming from the non-debtor spouse's attorney will say that this debt belongs to the debtor spouse, in perpetuity. Does that make sense? Going into mediation first gives the couple a chance to discuss this situation, ponder its implications, and think about how they want to handle the debt during their marriage. (See Chapter 6.)

Part of my mediation process is to put together a short list of six to eight attorneys I think would appropriately serve my clients for the next step. (See Chapter 20 for my method of finding attorneys.) The choice of attorneys is different for each set of clients. It depends on their personalities and the personalities and expertise of the lawyers.

Almost always I look for attorneys who practice collaborative law. The list of what kind of collaborative law attorneys I choose will be determined by what issues are primary to the prenup. If there are businesses involved, then I'd look for a collaborative law attorney experienced in business law. If there is high net worth and trusts in the picture, then I'd look for a collaborative law attorney with experience dealing with family wealth and trusts.

Ultimately, my clients and I will spend part of our last session looking at the websites of the attorneys. It's kind of a beauty pageant, and it's fun. I ask the clients for their sense of who their first and second choices would be.

Once they choose their attorneys, I have a Zoom session with both attorneys where I present the case, the background of the clients, the terms they chose, and the reasons they chose them. I review the term sheet with the attorneys. I also give them access to the clients' underlying financial documents that the clients provided, which are on a secure website. This gets the reviewing attorneys up to speed with the case. Because the financial documents and other facts have been gathered, and because there is already an agreed-to term sheet, the workload of the reviewing attorneys is lightened.

I speak with the attorneys about coordinating with each other regarding the drafting of the agreement. After speaking with their respective clients, the attorneys should create a single draft by going back and forth with each other, incorporating the term sheet provisions and any changes that have been agreed to by the clients. This way the clients get one final or almost-final draft rather than multiple "redlined" drafts. It's much easier for everyone involved. Once the mediation is complete, the attorney part of the process usually goes quickly and smoothly.

The cost of mediation plus attorney review is generally higher than the cost of engaging two attorneys at the outset. There are some savings, though, because the discussions in the mediation sessions and the development of a term sheet (which is the backbone of a prenuptial agreement) has already been done. As a result, the attorneys need to expend less time overall, which means fewer billable hours charged to their clients. But because of the nature of the mediation at the outset, it is a more open and collaborative (and even pleasant) experience for the couple. So even if the cost is somewhat higher using mediation first, my clients always say that the extra cost was worth it.

To find a prenup mediator, I suggest a Google search similar to the one that I presented in Chapter 20 for finding a prenup attorney. Because prenups are "law-heavy," the mediator should be an attorney, one who has a practice that includes (or included) divorce, estate-planning, and business law. The mediator, of course, should be experienced in the practice of mediation and should be experienced in prenuptial agreements.

The following search string should find some suitable mediators:

[your state] mediation collaborative law prenuptial agreement

Look at some of these attorneys' websites and think about what they say about themselves and their experience. The same deliberations that I described in how to choose an attorney (some of which are intangible feelings or reactions) apply to choosing a prenup mediator. By using the search string above and this method, you should be able to come up with some good options. Most attorneys and mediators now see clients using Zoom, so it doesn't matter in which part of your state the mediator (or your reviewing attorney) is located.

• • •

I hope this book has helped demystify the process of obtaining a prenup, explained options within a prenup for planning the financial part of a marriage, and given you a sense of the dangers and opportunities inherent in the process. Most of all, I hope this book has helped you on your journey in finding a prenup solution that will nourish and sustain your marriage.

ABOUT THE AUTHOR

Laurie Israel is a collaborative attorney and mediator based in Massachusetts. She is the author of *The Generous Prenup: How to Support Your Marriage and Avoid the Pitfalls* (2018) as well as this book, *The Marriage-Friendly Prenup: How to Create a Thoughtful and Caring Prenuptial Agreement*. Laurie concentrates her practice solely on prenuptial agreements and postnuptial agreements. She mediates and consults throughout the U.S. and represents clients in Massachusetts. Laurie has written extensively on prenups and the art and skill of mediating them. She believes that beginning the process with mediation is the optimal way to help couples mutually address the terms of a prenup and how the terms may affect their marriage and each of the spouses in the future.

Her writings and views on prenuptial agreements have appeared in *The New York Times*, *The Wall Street Journal*, *BBC,* and *The Huffington Post*. Laurie also has been interviewed by several other publications, including in *New York* magazine's "The Cut," and she frequently appears as a prenup expert on many podcasts.

Laurie began her involvement in this area of law as counsel for clients who were negotiating their prenuptial agreements. She experienced firsthand how couples can unintendingly harm each other during the usual attorney-led negotiation process in a way that may not easily be forgotten. Laurie believes that the content and process of many prenups does irreparable damage to the couple embarking on a marriage.

The primary message in *The Marriage-Friendly Prenup* is that prenups should not be taken lightly, should be used only when necessary, and should be used only when both parties are comfortable with the entire process and the result, which should be equitable to each of them. Laurie believes the professionals involved should be keenly aware of the issue of fairness to both parties and keep the ultimate health of the ensuing marriage of foremost concern in their approach.

Laurie's website is www.laurieisrael.com

ACKNOWLEDGMENTS

Many thanks to my friends, family, and colleagues who have encouraged me to write this new book on prenups, *The Marriage-Friendly Prenup: How to Create a Thoughtful and Caring Prenuptial Agreement*. They provided moral support throughout this project, and I am very grateful to them.

I especially thank the following people for their input on naming the book: Mary Dearborn, Eric Laursen, Venezia VanDerZyde, Bill Latimer, Alice Schertle, Roy Rudolph, Janice Wright, Linda Pilgrim, Ben Israel, Gabriela Franco Peña, and Elaine Sidney.

Working with narrator Nancy Gaines Bober on the Audible version of the book was a pleasure throughout, and I am pleased and grateful for the results. Thanks to Barbara Aronica for the book production and cover of both *The Marriage-Friendly Prenup* and *The Generous Prenup* and to Gabriela Franco Peña who designed the hyphen on the cover of the new book.

I would like to thank my family, Elaine, Ben, and Gaby, for their support and sound advice throughout the process of writing this new book. I also thank my legal assistant, Venezia VanDerZyde, for her talented and thoughtful editing of the manuscript; Bill Latimer, my second editor who combed the manuscript with a trained and elegant editor's eye; and Linda Pilgrim who capably and intelligently completed the final proofreading of the book, making improvements even after all our editing efforts, and burnishing the final product.

During the past several years, my practice has consisted solely of prenuptial agreement work, as an attorney, consultant, and mediator. I have learned a lot, gained great insight, and have become much better at my job. For this I thank my clients, who are courageous and intelligent. They always surprise me with their creativity in finding solutions. When I listen to their voices, I learn so much and grow in my job to more capably serve as counselor and neutral facilitator in this new field of creating humane and healthy prenups.

LEGAL DISCLAIMER

If you are embarking on having a prenuptial agreement (or postnuptial agreement) or are thinking about one, it is important that you retain a suitably qualified attorney licensed in your jurisdiction to assist you. The choice of an attorney is an important one that you must make carefully, based on your own judgment and evaluation of that attorney.

The material for this book is drawn from a composite of client situations. All identifying personal and factual information has been changed. Any resemblance to a particular individual's situation or any specific couple's situation is purely coincidental.

The contents of this book are presented for general information purposes only. This book cannot and does not take the place of legal advice by an attorney. It is intended only to provide information to readers interested in the topic of prenuptial agreements.

Use of this book does not create an attorney-client relationship between the author and the reader. The content and opinions expressed in this book are the opinions of the author only.

The information in this book may not be current, and the author cannot guarantee that the information is accurate or complete. The author makes no claims, promises, or guarantees about the accuracy, completeness, or adequacy of the information, opinions, and advice contained in this book.